ADAM CLAYTON POWELL

Portrait of a Marching Black

ADAM CLAYTON POWELL

Portrait of a Marching Black

by James Haskins

The Dial Press / New York

Library of Congress Cataloging in Publication Data
Haskins, James, 1941– Adam Clayton Powell: portrait of a marching Black.
Summary: A biography of the well-known black political figure whose
flamboyant conduct led to the denial of his seat in Congress.
Bibliography: p. 1. Powell, Adam Clayton, 1908–1972—Juvenile
literature. [Powell, Adam Clayton, 1908–1972. 2. Legislators.
3. Negroes—Biography] I. Title.
E748.P86H37   973.92′092′4 [B] [92]   73-6026
ISBN   0-8037-1809-8

To Adam Clayton Powell, IV

Foreword

One of my purposes in writing this book was to show something of Adam Clayton Powell, Jr., the man—a side that the public saw very rarely. Even in his own books he chose not to deal to any great extent with his own human side. In this book I hope I have succeeded in showing a different Adam Powell, whom very few people, except for relatives and his closest personal friends, saw. I have attempted to show Adam Powell, the man, from a variety of perspectives—how people in Harlem and Bimini saw him; how the average man in the street saw him; how people who knew him for many years and who worked closely with him remembered him.

In all the places I visited to get information on Adam

Powell, from the dirty, hopeless one-room End-of-the-World Bar on the island of Bimini to the impressive middle-class black apartments in Harlem to the bar stools in rotting hangouts on Seventh Avenue, the one thing that remained constant was the love of these people for Adam. It was a passionate love that seemed unshakeable, which probably explains his confidence over the years that the people of Harlem would never let him down; he knew in his heart that they loved him. Among the people I spoke to who were close to him in his last years was another constant—that he felt alone and deserted by those whom he loved and who had loved him. He was bewildered, depressed, angry, and yet somehow accepting of his fate. To the end, however, he refused to accept his loss to Charles Rangel in the 1970 congressional election, and there are a great many people in Harlem who felt and still feel that Powell did not actually lose. Even now, as I write, there must be thousands of blacks across the land who are giving a passing thought to or talking about Adam. To him, it is said, three-quarters of all black professionals in the '60s owed their jobs, either through the Federal Employment Practices Act or the Poverty Program.

There is a story I'd like to relate at this point. About three months before it occurred to me to write this book and before The Dial Press, which was Adam's publisher, decided to take it on, I was in an elevator in the garment district. Three black men got on; they were talking about the upcoming election between Livingston Wingate and Charles Rangel for Congress. One effectively ended the conversation when he said, "They are claiming a seat which is too hot for them both. Only one nigger ever sat in Congress who spoke for colored folk—Adam Powell—and he dead and gone." At that point I found myself saying, along with the other two men, "You're right about that." Such was the power of Adam Clayton Powell that at the sound of his name everyone listens.

When he was alive the one thing that all blacks had in political common in America was Adam Powell, and not to be lost in the elevator incident is the fact that these three men who wouldn't, I suppose, ordinarily be interested in politics were interested in Harlem and who represented her only because Adam had been King of Harlem. He was the very first to make the people of Harlem aware of their sleeping potential, of their manhood, of their pride, and for this, like Malcolm X, he could do no wrong. For this, he could go on European junkets and have wild parties and three wives and numerous girl friends and tell Congress and the world to go to hell. Adam was Our Man Flint, our man in Washington and, yes, when he went on those wild sprees of his we knew that we were with him, that Harlem was in Paris or London or deep-sea fishing and telling whitey where it's at.

James Haskins
New York, 1974

Many people are involved in the preparation of a book such as this. The greatest thanks, of course, are due those people whose recollections of Adam Powell, the man, are contained in the following pages; for their assistance, I am grateful to all of them. Thanks also to Margo Jefferson for transcribing the tapes and to Mary Ellen Arrington and Mary Ellen Agolia for typing the first and second manuscript drafts, and to Susan Kalhoefer for having typed the final manuscript, to Pat Connolly for helping with the editing, and to Ruth Ann Stewart for her helpful suggestions. A very special thanks to Kathy Benson.

ADAM CLAYTON POWELL

Portrait of a Marching Black

How do you measure greatness?

By the ageless beauty of the written word? By the inspiration of spoken eloquence?

Or does the eternal slide rule measure man's greatness by his deeds and legacy for generations to come? There is no simple formula.

But history will one day say of Adam Clayton Powell—"The noble acts which he did, and his greatness, they are not written: for they were very many."

Chuck Stone,
from the cover of Adam Clayton Powell's
album, Keep the Faith, Baby!

I

Bimini. The water is as blue and clear as in picture post-cards, and so shallow you can walk a mile till it rises past your knees. Palm trees, their spiky fronds rippling in the hot breeze, and hibiscus ablaze with orange and red blossoms. Coconuts, fallen from overladen palm trees, bake in the sun, and conch shells big as your head rest on the ocean floor. Nobody should go hungry on Bimini. How different is Adam Clayton Powell's last home from the dirty, tree-less streets of Harlem. But the people are black people, just as in Harlem, and Adam Powell used to say, "Where-ever there's black people, I'm home." And just like the black people of Harlem, when the people of Bimini saw the tall, light-skinned man come walking down the road, they knew he was not like the folks he resembled; they knew he was one of them.

Like most black people in the Western Hemisphere, Adam Clayton Powell, Jr. never knew who his African ancestors were or what his true surname might have been. Powell was the name of a German slaveowner in Virginia who died fighting to preserve slavery during the Civil War. It was not the name of the part-black, part-Cherokee Indian slave whom Powell impregnated; she had only a first name—Sally. Nor did Dunn, another slave of Powell's, who took the big-bellied Sally in and cared for her, have a last name. He did have a large *P* branded on his back, a punishment his master had administered after Dunn had tried to run away. Adam Clayton Powell, Jr. saw the little, dark-skinned Dunn only once, when he was ten years old, but he would ever after remember tracing the P-shaped scar on the bent back with his hand, and being told that was how he got his last name.

Sally, with the help of Dunn, brought Adam Clayton Powell, Jr.'s father into the world one night in 1865. It was not much of a world into which to bring a child. Dunn was very poor, so poor that Sally's son wore nothing but a shirt made from a bleached flour sack for the first seven years of his life. When he started school his mother wove a pair of trousers to go with the shirt. He did not have shoes.

School was a five-mile walk away, and the school year was short, lasting only until the end of March. In farming country no one went to school from planting time in April until the crops were harvested late in the summer. But despite the shortness of his first school year, Adam Powell learned to read, and he never stopped reading for the rest of his life.

In 1875 Dunn and Sally and her son, who was then ten, moved to West Virginia to work on the prospering tobacco farms. There, Adam Powell continued his schooling and met Mattie Schaefer, who would later become his wife. He also managed to get into every possible trouble a Negro boy in the South could get into. "During the eight years my father spent in West Virginia he was, according to his own account, a bum, a drunkard, a gambler, a juvenile delinquent, and possibly more," wrote Adam Powell, Jr. in his autobiography. "He always carried with him a pistol and a pair of brass knuckles, and had a jug of hard liquor on hand at all times." He got into so much trouble that in August of 1884, he had to leave town to keep from being murdered.

He traveled to Rendville, Ohio, a mining town, and took up where he had left off in West Virginia, gambling and collapsing on his bed every night in a drunken stupor. Who knows what might have become of Adam Powell, Sr., if he had not, one drunken night, thrown a shoe at what he thought was a window and broken his bedroom mirror? Discovering his error the next morning, he saw it as an omen. It was Sunday, and for the first time in years he went to church. It was a Baptist church, and it was holding a revival meeting. When Adam Powell walked out he was a church member, and a changed young man.

He returned to school, and upon graduation applied to Howard University Law School in Washington, D.C. He planned to go into law and then run for Congress. But Howard turned him down and he decided to go into the ministry instead. In 1888 he entered Wayland Seminary and College in Washington, D.C., graduating four years later with extremely high marks. Meanwhile he had returned to West Virginia for Mattie Schaefer, his childhood sweetheart. They were married in 1890.

In the fall of 1893, after an unhappy summer at Ebenezer Church in Philadelphia, the young couple moved to New Haven, Connecticut, where Powell had been offered the pastorship of Immanuel Baptist Church. The move proved to be a happy one. Powell's preaching drew huge crowds to the church and its membership increased rapidly. He began studying at Yale University and became secretary of the Baptist Ministers' Conference, whose chairman was George Barton Cutten. His salary was a good one for the time, and the parsonage was a large, comfortable, book-filled house on a tree-lined street. Into this comfortable, sheltered world, so very different from the world into which his father had been born, came Adam Clayton Powell, Jr. on November 29, 1908.

Adam Clayton Powell, Jr. lived in New Haven only for the first six months of his life. In the very month he was born, his father accepted the pastorship of Abyssinian Baptist Church on West 40th Street between Seventh and

Eighth avenues in New York City, the largest black congregation in the world. At first the Powells lived in a house far uptown on West 134th Street in Harlem. The area was almost totally white, populated by Jews, Irish, and Italians. The streets were lined with neat town houses; yards were surrounded by trees and shrubbery. Adam had every toy a child could want, a back yard to play in, and a room of his own as soon as he was old enough to move from the room adjacent to that of his parents. How different was his childhood from that of his father.

Adam was the baby of the family; the only other child, Blanche, was ten years old when Adam was born and she doted on him, as did his mother. The family housekeeper, Josephine, spoiled him as well; Reverend Powell was the only member of the family who at least claimed he didn't spoil his son. Blanche Powell married C. D. King when Adam was six years old, and from then on he was like an only child, enjoying the almost undivided attention of his parents.

"Often he'd tell us the story of how, when he was growing up, his mother would sit him upon a pile of soiled clothes while she was doing her washing and tell him stories from the Bible," says Hattie Dodson, who knew Adam Powell as a child and worked for his father and later for him at Abyssinian Baptist Church. "I'm sure he had some precious memories of his mother. I know when we were teenagers and his mother had been sick for a while, we were singing Christmas carols at the Powell

Adam Clayton Powell, Jr., three months old,
with his parents and his sister, Blanche

house on Christmas Eve. She had gotten out of bed and was sitting on the high step there, looking down at us. He never forgot that.

"His father used to take him to museums, and he would take him fishing a lot. That was one of the things that rubbed off on Adam—a love for fishing. Dr. Powell and two friends of his used to go deep-sea fishing in the Caribbean all during the winter. I think one of the places that his father took him when he was a youngster was Oak Bluffs on Martha's Vineyard in Massachusetts, and that was before there were many blacks up there."

The two would also fish at Carney Bay and Sheepshead Bay in Brooklyn. "They would leave home early in the morning, about 3:00 A.M.," remembers Adam's brother-in-law, C. D. King. "Dr. Powell would drive down there in his car. They would fish all day and then they would spend the night at a boarding house owned by some black people. They never had a boat; his father didn't even have his own car until he was an old man, must have been sixty."

As far back as he could remember, Adam would sit on his father's lap and listen while Reverend Powell read the Bible. He liked hearing the comforting drone of his father's voice, but he did not really understand the stories. As the elder Powell also read the Bible aloud before dinner, one would expect that Adam learned to read from the Bible, but this was not the case. He wrote in his autobiography, "The first influence on my education was Josephine, who, though only semiliterate, agonizingly taught me, when I was between three and four, the alphabet and how to read from the newspapers. On the long trolley car or elevated trips between our home on 134th Street and the church on 40th Street, Josephine taught me not only to read my *ABC*'s but to print them." From then on, like his father before him, Adam never stopped reading.

"He read a lot," C. D. King recalls. "In order to stop him from reading his mother would have to turn the lights out in his bedroom; but he would just take a flashlight and read under the bedcovers where no one could see him. Mostly, he read his father's books; his father did not have much fiction, so Adam read serious books. He was always a studious type because of the way he grew up."

Adam skipped to the second term of the first grade shortly after he began the first term. Thereafter, he skipped term after term, graduating from high school when he was sixteen.

"He was not much of a boy's boy," says C.D. King. "He was the heart of his mother. He climbed trees, but he wasn't at all wild; in fact he was rather tame. He wasn't much of an athlete, never fought or carried on, and he wouldn't get into a ruckus if there was any way to avoid it."

There was a reason for Adam's being "rather tame." In 1914, when he was not quite six, Adam became seriously ill with a lung condition, and for the next six years his parents invested nearly all their money and energy in keeping him alive. These were years of not being allowed to play strenuous games with other children, of being carried from one spot to another, of sitting in the sun on park benches with his mother, of being protected from germs. For the rest of his life Adam would be susceptible to respiratory diseases.

His illness notwithstanding, however, Adam did come close to being a sissy, at least in appearance. "Josephine always fixed my pale-yellow hair in curls. Yes, curls! I wore Little Lord Fauntleroy suits, Buster Brown collars, and flowing black ties. . . . I even had a gray Persian lamb coat for the winter. And my hat! The first time I went to Venice and saw the gondoliers, I said, 'They have my childhood hat.' Yes, they were exactly alike—broad brimmed with streamers. And I wore patent leather shoes. No wonder when Roi Ottley saw me for the first time, being led by Josephine, very much the governess in her correct uniform, he turned to W. C. Handy, Jr. and said, 'My God, is that a boy or a girl?' I was apparently the only one in the family who knew what I was with unmistakable conviction."

When Roi Ottley, who would later become a well-known black author, first saw Adam, the Powell family had just returned to Harlem after living for two years in a tenement near Abyssinian Baptist Church on West 40th Street. Their new home was on West 136th Street. By that time, about 1918, Harlem was beginning to change. More blacks were moving in, and naturally there was tension between the Irish, who were called "Micks," and the blacks. Adam had not been very conscious of race in his short life. The comfortable circumstances of his family had helped shield him from the racism experienced by poorer blacks, and as the reverend's son he had enjoyed a special status at school. But back in Harlem he learned about racism from both blacks and whites.

"The first night my father sent me out to buy the evening paper in our new neighborhood, on 136th Street, a gang of Negro boys grabbed me and asked, 'What are you, white or colored?' I had never thought of color. I looked at my skin and said, 'White!' Whereupon I was promptly and thoroughly beaten. The very next night I had to go to Eighth Avenue to get something from the store for Mother, and a gang of white boys grabbed me and demanded, 'What are you?' Remembering my answer, and my beating of the preceding night, I answered, 'Colored!' Whereupon I again was bloodied. On the third night, another group of colored boys grabbed me on Seventh Avenue and asked the same question, 'What are you?' Remembering once more my previous experiences, I said, 'Mixed!' One of the boys yelled out, 'Oh, he's a Mick!' And I was sent home crying for a third time." It was hard for Adam to understand how the color of one's skin could be so important, and harder for him to figure out how to avoid being beaten up by both sides.

Eventually the black youths would gain the upper hand in the struggle for the streets of Harlem by sheer force of numbers. By the early 1920s the business boom created by World War I was drawing thousands of Southern blacks North in search of jobs and to Harlem in search of living quarters. The Reverend Powell could see that more would come, and he decided the Abyssinian should go where the black people needed it. After all, it had been founded by and for black people.

Gwen Jones has spent most of her life working in Abyssinian Baptist Church and she has great reverence for what it represents. "It's an historic Baptist church, started by a group of Ethiopians who were not slaves, but rich merchants. They came to New York and found that they would have to sit in the gallery of the First Baptist Church downtown. So they set up their own church and named it after their homeland. Ethiopia was once named Abyssinia. Dr. Powell, too, was a pioneer in his way; he brought it to Harlem, opened it up to everybody."

It was not easy for the Reverend Powell to convince his congregation of the desirability of moving to Harlem. He had first begun talking about the move in 1911, but the church didn't purchase the land for a new building until 1920. The land was on 138th Street between Seventh and Lenox avenues. On it Reverend Powell pitched a large tent and for two summers held services every single night. Thousands packed the tent night after night, church membership increased to four thousand, the church treasury filled. The money was spent on the new church buildings.

Hattie Dodson, who grew up in the church says, "I understand that the site they chose was covered by a huge rock, and the rock was blasted and the church was made from that rock."

To young Adam the new church was a marvelous, wonderful thing, and he had been a part of it from the very beginning. "I helped to clear the land upon which the first tent was pitched. The land was cleared by volunteers from the church, and while they worked the ladies served them food. I ran back and forth with a pail of lemonade to refresh them as they toiled under the hot sun. Though still a boy, I helped to drive the first peg that put the guys of the tent in place. I stood by my father as the masons laid the cornerstone. I helped plan the gymnasium of the community center. Every step of the way I was part of the building of that Tudor–Gothic structure, even to running downstairs sometimes, late at night, to throw the switches that turned off lights the sexton had left burning. This was my church. It was my eternal mother."

Adam was fifteen when the new church buildings were dedicated in June of 1923. He had recovered from his sickly condition, had put on weight, and was showing promise of matching his father's 6-foot-3-inch, 190-pound frame. He was attending Townsend Harris preparatory school for the College of the City of New York. Only students with an elementary school average of *A* were accepted at Townsend, which was a three-year high school, and if a student could get through Townsend he was automatically accepted at C.C.N.Y. Adam made the basketball team and earned his first letter there, which indicates just how well he had recovered from his sickly period. Partly due to his urging, a basketball team was formed in Abyssinian's gymnasium, and for years the team won all the championships of the Inter-Church Athletic League.

"Basketball in those days was very different from

basketball today," Adam Powell wrote later. "It was not a competition for giants, with an adding machine needed to keep score. There was one tall man to jump center, two short, fast people we called ponies to play forwards, and two heavier men to play guards. Games rarely went over thirty-five or forty points. We wore long stockings and big leather kneepads."

Adam caught the interest of C.C.N.Y.'s physical education director and basketball coach, who urged him to go to C.C.N.Y. after graduation. Adam had not thought seriously about where he wanted to go to college, but C.C.N.Y. was free for residents of New York; so upon graduation from Townsend he enrolled in the college.

But Adam barely graduated from high school, his grades were so poor. Basketball was one reason, girls were another. Adam fell in love for the first time during his first year at Townsend when he was thirteen, and from then on his social life got better and better and his grades became worse and worse. The pattern continued at C.C.N.Y.

"The girls liked him very much," C. D. King remembers. "From the time he was fifteen or sixteen they really began to go for him. When he went to City College he was getting to be something of a playboy, so he didn't do so well. Going to parties, smoking, drinking, chasing and being chased by girls, and generally having a good time caused Adam to flunk three subjects his first term. Ordinarily he would have been flunked out of college, but Dr.

Powell knew the president of the school and used his influence to allow Adam to return the second semester."

Dr. Powell made it clear to his son that his patience was sorely tried. He had always been so proud of his son and of his son's success in school. He could not understand the change that had come over Adam—the wildness, the carelessness, the irresponsibility. "He did not remember his teenage experiences as a bum, a gambler, and a drunkard back in Rendville, Ohio," Adam later wrote. "And I, not knowing at that time he had gone through a similar period in his own life, rebelled against his 'holier-than-thou' attitude and his 'Calvinism.' "

It was a difficult time for the entire Powell family, and the relationship between Adam and his father became more and more strained. And then, during his second semester at C.C.N.Y, Adam's sister Blanche died of a ruptured appendix at the age of twenty-seven. "That was the end . . . of college, of church, and of faith! Whereas I had gotten three F's in the first semester at C.C.N.Y., I got five F's in the second. I was kicked out. My father washed his hands of me. My sister was dead. And I just didn't give a damn!"

Adam had idolized his sister; although ten years separated their ages, he had always felt an unusual closeness to her. "There were only two of them," C. D. King explains. "She was ten years older than he, but she was the only sister he had and he was very attached to her." When Adam was six, Blanche had married C. D. King who then moved into the family home, but she had been very young when she married, and after five or six years there had been a divorce. Adam was only ten or eleven at the time and he had welcomed the return of his adored sister. Although she later remarried, the two remained close, and it was to Blanche that he had turned during the stormy time with his parents. Blanche understood Adam's viewpoint, and he had come to depend upon her as he had depended upon his parents before. With her death he felt he had no one, and for a time he went wild—losing jobs as fast as he got them, spending money, getting drunk, having girls. He was going nowhere and he knew it, but he didn't care.

Adam's parents cared. They sought the advice of a family friend, who suggested that Adam be sent to Colgate University, a small, all-male college in upstate New York, thirty-five miles from the nearest town. There he would be away from the bad influence of girls and parties. There, perhaps, he would straighten out.

Adam Clayton Powell, Sr. personally drove his son to Colgate that fall and was met with a surprise. The president of the college was none other than George Barton Cutten, who seventeen years earlier, in New Haven, had been chairman of the Baptist Ministers' Conference of which Dr. Powell had been secretary. Although Dr. Cutten must have known the Powells were Negro, he apparently did not mention the fact to others at the college. At Colgate in the 1920s each new student was placed in a dormitory room with another student chosen at random by the university. At least that was the system for placing new white students. Black students, of which there were only a few, were specially placed with other black students. When Adam Powell arrived at Colgate, he was placed in a room with a white student, and it did not take him long to realize that his racial background was unknown. The mistake was easily understood; Colgate is far away from New York City and the name Powell did not mean anything special to the students or the administration. Then, too, Adam Powell looked white. Adam did not point out the mistake to anyone, and when fraternity pledging season arrived he pledged a white fraternity.

That spring Reverend Powell was invited to be a guest chapel speaker. Chapel was compulsory at Colgate, and guests often spoke there. Reverend Powell was a fine speaker and a commanding presence, and the students enjoyed hearing him speak. He chose as his subject the plight of the Negro, and his words were very forceful and moving. The feeling with which he pleaded the Negro cause, however, caused some of the students to suspect that he must be a Negro himself, and if Dr. Powell was a Negro then so was Adam. When Adam returned to his dormitory room that day he found a note from his roommate. The two had been very good friends but now his roommate wanted Adam out of the room. The dean of students made no attempt to defend Adam, and for a time many students and faculty members would hardly speak to him. Fortunately, one unprejudiced philosophy teacher understood how difficult the situation was for Adam and counseled him until the incident passed. From this Adam learned that one does not choose what he is going to be in a society like America's—society chooses for him. What one does choose is how he is going to feel and act about the choice society makes. It was a hard lesson to learn.

Despite this incident, Adam's years at Colgate were not unhappy. He and his friends would drive five miles to the nearest tavern to drink beer laced with hard liquor. They stole alcohol from the chemistry lab and mixed it with ginger ale. They knew every farmer for miles around who manufactured homemade corn liquor. They played craps and poker and got into as much trouble as possible without getting caught. Getting caught drunk would have led to immediate expulsion. During summers Adam worked at various resorts. His parents never mentioned the expense of sending him to Colgate, and he never had to work while attending school, but his father insisted he work every summer. One summer he worked at Equinox House in Vermont, and there he learned more about racism.

"The son of Abraham Lincoln, Robert Todd Lincoln, drove up to the Equinox House nightly for dinner. He hated Negroes and whenever a Negro put his hand on the car door to open it, Mr. Lincoln took his cane and cracked him across the knuckles. The manager asked me if, at a special increase in salary, I would take care of Mr. Lincoln's car each night when it arrived. So promptly every day, when Robert Todd Lincoln's chauffered car rolled up with the son of the former President of the United States, I, whose father had been raised by a branded slave, would open his door. And Mr. Lincoln, looking at my white hand, was satisfied. For the service I received $1 a day from him and $10 a week from the inn's management."

Adam continued his wild ways throughout his years at Colgate, going out with all kinds of girls, gambling, drinking. Toward the end of his years at Colgate, Adam and a friend who owned a car, began driving down to New York City every weekend. During one of these weekends, Adam met Isabel Washington, a young actress and dancer who was separated from her husband and had a child. Dr. Powell strongly disapproved of the relationship and let Adam know in no uncertain terms just what he thought of his son going around with a married, older woman who was in the theater.

All in all, though, Dr. Powell was pleased with his son. In his second year at Colgate, Adam's marks had begun to improve, and his record for the last three years of college had been outstanding. In his senior year, he decided to apply to the Harvard Medical School and become a doctor, and of course his parents were happy. His father had planned to go into law, until God talked to him. Adam would have become a doctor, but God talked to him.

It happened late one night in the second half of his senior year. He distinctly heard a soft, insistent voice saying, "Whom shall I send? Who will go for me?"

Adam had never thought seriously about going into the ministry, even though he had been involved with it for most of his life, even though as a small boy he had sat on the church dais next to his father and felt the importance of being "up there." His parents had never tried to persuade him to enter the ministry. Yet that night Adam decided to follow in the footsteps of his father. When he called home the next morning to tell of his decision, his parents were overjoyed.

Adam Clayton Powell, Jr. preached his first sermon on Good Friday night that spring of 1930. On that night the crowd that filled Abyssinian Baptist Church was slightly more varied than usual. "All the girls from the Cotton Club, others from the downtown night clubs, girls of every color, bootleggers, gamblers, all the fantastic array of acquaintances I had accumulated through the years," Adam recalled later. "I can still remember the sight. They all came to laugh. 'Adam's going to preach!' "

"When he preached his first sermon," says Adam's brother-in-law, C. D. King, "he chose as his text, an advertisement for a cigarette, 'I'd walk a mile for a Camel; how far will you walk for God?' That was very unusual, he didn't take any text from the Bible, he took that cigarette ad. Most of his sermons were just about life. He said in that sermon that being a preacher would not change him, that he might do it better but he wasn't going to change."

The following week Dr. Powell and the deacons of the

Adam Clayton Powell, Jr.,
at his graduation from Colgate

church granted Adam a license to preach. They also made it clear that the job of business manager and assistant to his father would be waiting for him in the fall. Also shortly thereafter, Adam applied to and was accepted at Union Theological Seminary.

Immediately after graduating from Colgate in June of 1930, Adam set off on a trip to Europe. The elder Powell had been planning to give his son a trip abroad as a graduation present anyway, but by graduation time he saw the trip also as a means of getting Adam to forget Isabel Washington, whom he was seeing despite his decision to enter the ministry.

"The purpose of the trip," C. D. King recalls, "was as much to get his mind off this girl as for the experience of traveling. His father made him promise that he would not get in touch with her the whole time he was away, but Adam cabled her the first day out at sea. The old man just couldn't break it up."

For nearly four months Adam traveled in Europe, Egypt, and the Holy Land. Perhaps seeing the rich civilizations of black people in Egypt and the Holy Land gave him a greater pride in and understanding of his black heritage, just as a similar trip did Malcolm X half a century later. But during his absence events were taking place which would have even more effect on his life. Back home the Depression had hit, causing great suffering to black people in America.

Adam returned from his four-month trip abroad eager to work in the church and eager to develop his credentials for the ministry through study. He entered New York City's Union Theological Seminary. An old and respected institution, it was not known to be conservative; in fact one reason why Adam chose to go there was its reputation for liberalism. Not long after Adam enrolled there, however, he began to question this reputation. Union's president, Dr. Henry Sloane Coffin, disapproved strongly of Adam's relationship with Isabel Washington and actively tried to persuade Adam to stop seeing her. Adam listened respectfully but kept on seeing Isabel; he felt that whom he dated was none of Dr. Coffin's business. Dr. Coffin's unwanted advice irked Adam, but it was a later incident which caused him to put an end to his studies at Union. He had written a prayer for Dr. Coffin's prayer class, and it had been returned to him marked, "Of no value." Adam did not feel that any man had the right to judge another man's words to God as being of no value.

Union Seminary was not for him nor, he decided, were straight theological studies. Feeling that the study of religious education would be of more value to his work in the church, he enrolled in Columbia University's Teachers College. There he studied not just his own but other religions as well, which he felt gave him a broader understanding of religion in the world. He received a Master's degree in religious education from Teachers College.

Earning his Master's degree was quite a feat, for Adam attended classes at Teachers College while carrying a heavy work load at Abyssinian—more than most young men his age could have handled. The Depression was worsening, and for black people especially those countless jobs created by World War I had vanished in the postwar crash. People were starving, losing hope; they needed their church now more than ever before.

There was so much to do, so many who needed help. Dr. Powell started a community center in the basement of the church, opening its doors to anyone who needed shelter whether they were church members or not. He was criticized greatly for doing so, but he wanted to do all he could to help. Until Adam returned, the elder Powell had been carrying alone the burden of helping the people of the community, and soon after Adam arrived he suffered a nervous breakdown. His doctor ordered complete rest and total freedom from worry; if the elder Powell was to recover he must not even be allowed to think of work. The illness could not have come at a more difficult time.

Adam had been working at the church for only a few weeks and already he had made his presence felt. Although it was not an official title, he was often called junior pastor, and to many young members of the church he had become the pastor.

Hattie Dodson remembers the special relationship he had with these young members: "At that time the young people really began to go to church. It was downstairs that Adam spoke (he wasn't known as Mr. Powell or Reverend Powell, but just plain Adam) and all the people used to flock there. There was such a wonderful friendly feeling, and the services were so interesting that a lot of the adults started going down there." The young people could relate to Adam better than to his father; he spoke their language and he talked about the real world.

Lewis Upshur, who later became one of Adam's most active political workers and a close friend, did not really like Adam until he heard him preach. He thought Adam was flamboyant and somewhat conceited, although he really did not know the young assistant minister very well. He went to Abyssinian to hear Adam one Sunday partly in order to prove to himself that Adam could not preach. But after hearing the sermon Upshur changed his mind. "Adam said that the white people always tell us to look

Powell's father, the Reverend Adam
Clayton Powell, with Mrs. Powell

up and say, 'God is upstairs—' 'You don't see nothing up there,' he said. 'Everything is on earth. Gold, iron—the white man doesn't ever want the black man to notice anything that is in the earth. He's just supposed to look up where he can't see anything. There's a God, but have you ever seen him up there?' And I loved him from then on, and I've been following him ever since."

Still, Adam Powell was only twenty-one years old and had preached just a few sermons when his father became ill. He had never shouldered any great responsibilities and was immature in many ways. The church deacons must have pondered his youth and inexperience when they found Abyssinian without a pastor. But they expected him to follow in his father's footsteps and become pastor someday, and they appointed him acting minister. Suddenly Adam found himself responsible for the largest black church in the country and for a huge congregation many of whom were jobless and starving.

The first winter was a very difficult one for Adam Powell, Jr., but it was also a winter of great personal growth. He saw the long relief lines, the crowds of domestic workers standing on street corners willing to work for ten cents an hour, the hungry coatless children shivering in the cold. He understood for the first time what it must be like to be poor, really poor, and he realized that something more had to be done by the church. Dinner was traditionally served after church service (Adam knew that was the reason church attendance didn't drop off that winter; his sermons were not as good as his father's), but starving people couldn't get by on one hot meal a week. And what about the 63 per cent of the school children in Abyssinian's neighborhood who went to school hungry? Adam set up a free food kitchen, organized clothing drives, opened the doors of Abyssinian to anyone who needed shelter.

Hattie Dodson was among those who volunteered to help. She recalls, "We had a clothing depot downstairs and one day this big fellow came in and I looked down at his feet—his shoes had no bottoms, just tops, and it was winter. I did not have any shoes that would fit him, but Adam was big and I called upstairs, 'Adam! I have a man down here that has no shoes on. And it's cold.' He called back, 'You're telling me—I've only got two pairs myself.' But then he said, 'Wait a minute,' and he sent down one of his pairs of shoes for the man. Anytime I needed anything for a big man I'd call Adam and he would share his things. He was like that."

Busy as he was, Adam knew the church was only engaging in a holding action, merely keeping food in hungry stomachs and coats on shivering bodies. Then, in the early part of 1931, Adam Powell was visited by five black doctors. They had just been fired from Harlem Hospital for no other reason than they were black, and they asked his help in getting their jobs back. In Harlem Hospital where 90 per cent of the patients were black, why should all the doctors be white? Five white doctors had needed jobs, so five black doctors were fired to make room for them. And wasn't that why so many other black people in

Harlem had lost their jobs in the Depression? Wasn't it black people who were always fired first? Adam had known that just putting food into empty stomachs wasn't enough; now he realized something had to be done to prevent those stomachs from being empty in the first place. Something had to be done to keep black people from losing their jobs.

"What can I do?" Adam asked.

"Organize the people to help us get our jobs back," the doctors answered.

So Adam called together as many people as he could and formed the Committee on Harlem Hospital. They picketed the hospital, tried to see its superintendent, met with the commissioner of hospitals of the city of New York, but their efforts were of no avail. It was frustrating not to be listened to, not to be taken seriously. Slowly Adam realized that the problem was that black people had no power. They had to have a position of strength to bargain from; but it couldn't come from money, for black people had no money, and it couldn't come from political power, for black people had no political power. The one strength the black people of Harlem had was numbers, so that was the strength Adam and his group would use.

In the spring of 1931 Adam and the rest of the Committee on Harlem Hospital called for a mass protest by black people at City Hall. They posted signs throughout the community and announced it in church and at meetings. But they did not know how many Harlemites would answer the call. All they could do was hope for a good turnout and hope that the people who did come would not be frightened away by the several hundred riot police visibly stationed in the City Hall area. They realized that the mass protest could turn out to be a demonstration to which nobody came.

"I was the first to arrive at City Hall," Adam later recalled, "with just the two or three others who rode down in the car with me. We stood on the sidewalk and waited. Suddenly—up from the subways . . . down from the elevated lines . . . and out of the buses . . . our people streamed. We had expected a few hundred, but after the first thousand arrived, we had to move from the sidewalks into City Hall Park. Then two or three thousand more came. I had to stand on a bench and finally on top of a car in order to talk to them. There were six thousand people marching together; they were my people, and I belonged to them. On this day we stepped up the tempo of democracy in action in New York City."

The Board of Estimate was in session and though the police tried to bar Powell from the room in which they were meeting, he demanded to be heard. Once inside he spoke not only of the unfairness of the firing of the five doctors but of the unfairness of a hospital serving blacks but staffed and run by whites and of its generally unsanitary and deplorable conditions. The members of the board listened to this fiery twenty-two year old, and they listened well. As a result of that meeting, Harlem Hospital was given a complete overhaul: its staff was made truly interracial, a black doctor was made medical director, unsanitary conditions were cleaned up, and many other reforms were introduced.

That was the beginning. That was the day when Adam Powell realized that black people could do something to change the conditions of their lives. That was the day when he realized that what he wanted to do for the rest of his life was to help them improve their lives, and from then on Adam Powell never stopped fighting for black people.

The City Hall demonstration received wide publicity, and so did its leader, Adam Powell. As the Depression grew worse and worse, the plight of Harlem's poor had become more and more obvious to the outside community, but most people felt there was nothing they could do. At that time, during the early 1930s, there was no Department of Public Welfare in New York City; in fact no city or state agencies were equipped to cope with the effects of the Depression. After Adam led the people of Harlem to City Hall, however, two wealthy financiers, Seward Prosser and Harvey Gibson, were so impressed that they contacted him to offer their help.

This was in 1932, Adam was not quite twenty-four, but he met with the men in a splendid Wall Street office and boldly asked for as much money as they could give, not for handouts, not for giveaways, but for work that the people of Harlem could do. They gave it, and with it, as well as with money from his father, Adam set up the largest relief bureau ever established for blacks. With this money and donations from food markets, he expanded Abyssinian's free food kitchen to feed a thousand people a day. And to the many other facets of Abyssinian's program he added an employment committee. He had told the two business-men that he would not be giving out handouts. He knew the people of Harlem wanted jobs, and he was determined to find as many jobs as he could.

"He said, 'We're going to find jobs; we are going to make up a committee to find jobs,' " Hattie Dodson re-calls. "And of course all the young people fell right into line. They came to the church to work and anywhere we could put people to work we did. We contacted stores and businesses, but many of these jobs required skills, so natu-rally the church turned into a school. There were classes in typing, shorthand, economics, French, plastering, paint-ing, everything. I think Adam learned his ability to or-ganize from his father. His father was a great organizer." Later, in the mid-1930s, New York City would set up its first Department of Public Welfare, but it was not nearly so well organized or effective as the relief program at Abyssinian Baptist Church.

Adam was twenty-four years old, and he had more power than most forty year olds. The people of Abyssin-ian Baptist Church liked him and praised his relief work, yet they still had reservations about his youth and about the young woman he had refused to forget. In the years since they had first met, many changes had occurred in the lives of both Isabel Washington and Adam Powell. Isabel's career had blossomed, taking her away from New York often on tours and engagements. Adam had become intensely involved in the affairs of Abyssinian Baptist Church. Yet they continued to see one another, and in the early 1930s Adam squired Isabel to more and more church functions. Dr. and Mrs. Powell had tried everything possible to bring an end to the relationship, and the church elders had made it clear to Adam that marriage to a divorced woman in show business would be completely unacceptable. A man of his position should marry someone like a doctor's daughter. But Adam was determined to make his own decisions, and in 1933 he married Isabel.

The fears of the elder Powells and the congregation subsided as Isabel gave up her career completely and plunged into church activities. Perhaps, they even began to hope, Isabel would prove to have a calming influence upon her husband. For although they applauded his efforts to relieve the suffering caused by the Depression and praised his growing preaching abilities, many of the elder members of the congregation could not overlook his flamboyance and his penchant for doing the town. They just did not feel he conducted himself in a sufficiently dignified manner.

Lillian Upshur, who eventually became one of the chief political leaders for Adam in Harlem, recalls his early flamboyance. "He always liked an entourage—oh, he loved to be surrounded by people. When they saw him some people would say, 'Here comes the Pied Piper.' One night when he'd been back in New York about three or four years, I was in the Red Rooster, and all of a sudden here comes Adam with about five people in tow. He said to the bartender, 'Lock the door,' and then turned around and announced, 'Everybody in, stay in; everybody out, stay out.' He bought drinks for everyone in the bar. He always liked being the center of attention."

Sometimes, newcomers to his entourage, those who did not really know him, could become so caught up in the magic aura that surrounded Adam Powell that they would forget whom they were with. They would be surprised and puzzled by his sudden change of mood when a serious matter arose.

"When he was taking care of business it was strictly business," says Lillian Upshur. "If he was talking and there was some disruption, he would really be angry, and you had to remember what he was saying. He used to say, 'I don't listen with my mouth, I listen with my ears.' "

Behind the veneer of "good-time flamboyance" there was an intense seriousness in Adam Clayton Powell, Jr.

III

Abyssinian Baptist Church had become a huge relief center, and yet all of its activities could not blunt the cutting edge of the Depression, which went on and on. It seemed impossible that the situation of the people of Harlem could become any more miserable, but it did, and the frustration and anger of the people smoldered. A single spark could ignite the entire community, and in March, 1937, it came.

A Puerto Rican boy had been caught stealing in a five-and-ten-cent store and the white manager had beaten him. The story spread throughout the community, and suddenly the flames roared. Harlemites looted and burned the community's stores, hurled bricks at the police, shouted and cursed and released all their pent-up frustrations in a night of wild rioting. When the cold light of dawn broke the next morning, four were dead, scores injured, and a quarter of a million dollars' worth of property damaged. The people of Harlem were exhausted, and no better off than they had been before.

A kind of riot occurred inside Adam Clayton Powell, too. Why had this happened? Why had the people burned and looted their own community? Why had that particular incident set off such a night of destruction? He struggled inside himself to find out why, and, suddenly, it all seemed clear. Why had they looted and burned their own community? Because it wasn't really their community. They lived in it, but whites owned it. Whites owned the stores; whites worked in those stores; whites took home the money blacks spent in those stores. Powell made a survey of the entire length of 125th Street, the main thoroughfare of Harlem, and found that of some five thousand people who worked on that street only ninety-three were black, and all ninety-three were floor washers and sidewalk sweepers—no clerks, no managers, not even any waitresses. According to Adam's long-time friend Lewis Upshur, two other men had protested against the refusal of the 125th Street stores to employ representative numbers of blacks. "They started it, but the white men began to pay them off, and when the white men began to pay them off Adam went in and took up the fight himself." Within a few days after the riot, Adam had organized the Coordinating Committee for Employment. Its purpose was to make all those businesses that took black people's money give them jobs in return.

Realizing they would need the support of the black community, the committee, under Adam's leadership, appealed for support and received it. "He had a certain magnetism that drew people to him," comments Lillian Upshur, who also worked in the church at that time. "He just announced that he was going to have a meeting at the Golden Gate, and that place holds three thousand people. It's a ballroom, but it turned out to be a sort of town meeting hall. Adam made the announcement of the meeting, and people came out in the thousands, some even had to stand. The people were aroused, ready to be led; they recognized his leadership and of course he already had a large base of support in the church itself."

There were some black organizations that would not support the cause. Their spokesmen said, "Your cause is good, but your intention to boycott and picket these businesses is too militant." Thus many moderate black organizations did not send representatives to the committee. A. Philip Randolph (who had organized the Brotherhood of Sleeping Car Porters, the Harlem Chapter of the National Association for the Advancement of Colored People, the Harlem Labor Union, and other organizations) did support the cause, and with his support the committee began to organize its protests. Their slogan was, Don't buy where you can't work, and with this standard the committee set up picket lines in front of half the stores on 125th Street. At first some people in the community continued to shop in those stores, but soon it became a disgrace for any black person to cross the picket lines. The small, family-owned-and-operated businesses gave in quickly; the large chain stores were another matter. They could afford a few weeks of poor business as long as other chain stores in Harlem were doing poorly also. Realizing this, Adam suggested that the committee concentrate on just one of several chain stores that carried similar merchandise. They would picket Grant's, for example, and leave Woolworth's alone. Eventually, Grant's would give in and then the committee would picket Woolworth's. Woolworth's would give in because if it did not all the black business would go to Grant's.

"I was involved in the picketing," Lillian Upshur recalls. "We picketed the stores for a number of weeks until the big stores on 125th Street began to negotiate, and then of course things changed. It wasn't immediate, but it was pretty fast. Before, we weren't able to go to the theater and sit anyplace we wanted to—we had to sit in the back, in the balcony—but after the protest we could sit where we pleased."

Just getting the businesses in Harlem to agree to hire blacks was not enough; it was necessary to make sure there were blacks who were qualified for the jobs. At that time most stores, in Harlem as well as downtown, had training programs for their prospective employees; if a person did not do well in the program he did not get the job. To help insure that black people would get the jobs, Lillian Upshur relates, "We trained people in the Y, showing them how to speak to customers, how to handle sales, every phase of salesmanship. Many of those we helped were employed in the stores. Then of course we wanted to go on to bigger things, so Adam decided we would go to the telephone company and the gas and electric company."

The committee's strategy for bringing about an end to discrimination in employment practices in New York's public utilities was simple. Blacks picketed the utility company, and when merely picketing didn't work they declared every Tuesday a lightless night. The Harlem stores then appealed to the utility company: "We simply cannot turn out our night lights, we will be robbed," they insisted. Before long, the utility company had integrated its employees. The next target was the telephone company, which had just instituted a dial system. The committee picketed the company's downtown offices and also threatened to have everyone in Harlem pick up his telephone at the same time and dial Operator. The telephone company's young dialing system couldn't take that, and soon the telephone company was integrated.

All through the late 1930s and early 1940s the people of Harlem, led by Adam Clayton Powell, attacked the bastions of segregation, including the New York World's Fair Corporation. The slogan of the 1939 World's Fair was, *Building the World of Tomorrow*, and Adam told the president, Grover Whalen, "You cannot have a world of tomorrow from which you have excluded black people."

Whalen answered, "I do not see why the world of today

or tomorrow of necessity has to have colored people playing an important role."

Adam later recalled, "For the first time we moved our picket line downtown, picketing the Empire State Building, where the New York World's Fair Corporation had its headquarters. Every Thursday night we held a death watch. It was there, on those all-night death watches, that unity reached out and brought into the ranks more 'makers of the dream.' Chorus girls from Ethel Waters' Broadway hit would come to walk the picket line at midnight; the Cotton Club girls would come over between shows; the first Negro General Sessions Judge of the City of New York, Miles Paige, picketed every Thursday night. As a result of this picketing we received close to six hundred jobs at the World's Fair."

The next target was the city's bus corporation, which refused to hire any blacks except as cleaners in the garages. It was 1941 and the white drivers were beginning their own campaign to unionize the company. Adam quickly saw that the drivers and black people could help each other. He arranged a meeting with the head of the Transport Workers Union, Mike Quill.

"If you will support me after you have won your organization drive, then I will support you now," Adam said to Quill, and he agreed. Adam later wrote in his autobiography, "On March 10, I received a phone call from Quill saying that the twelve-day-old strike was finished and that the settlement announcement would be made in a few hours. Five hours after the Transport

Workers Union's victory had been announced, we struck. . . . Our signs read: 'We stayed off these buses for twelve days that white men might have a decent standard of living. Keep on staying off them now for the rights of black men.' We had seventy pickets the first night, nine hundred one week later, two thousand the third week. In the fourth week, when we began to send thousands of pickets downtown, the company began to weaken. The white bus drivers refused to drive through Harlem—not out of fear, but because we helped them in their own days of campaigning. From 110th Street south along Fifth Avenue, Eighth Avenue, every avenue, hundreds of buses were left vacant, night after night."

What could the bus company do? It would go bankrupt without Harlem's business. Before long, many black drivers were steering those buses, and black people went back to riding on them.

"And when we had gotten all those companies to open up to blacks, we formed what we called the People's Committee. Adam was the chairman, and one Saturday a month we would meet and discuss problems," says Gwen Jones, who had long been a member of Abyssinian Baptist Church and who was hired by Adam to work in the community center of Abyssinian. "After the picketing was over we began using a new method—negotiation. We would have conferences and we were able to open up, through Adam, a lot of jobs blacks had never been able to hold: certain hospital jobs and jobs in private industries like the beer companies—members of my family benefited from all this."

With each new success, more and more people joined the cause, and there were very few residents of Harlem who did not walk at least one picket line during those years. Anyone who offered support was welcome. Powell and his movement were criticized strongly for accepting the support of the American Communist Party, but he argued that what was needed were numbers and if he could get numbers from the Communist Party then they were welcome.

By 1941, Adam Powell had become one of the most powerful leaders in Harlem. He had a strong power base as pastor of Abyssinian Baptist Church, a deep well of support among the people because of his inroads against job segregation, and a weekly column in Harlem's news-paper, the *Amsterdam News,* in which he wrote of the op-pression of black people. He had come a long way from his college days when he had searched for a career and a goal; now he had one, and he was completely committed to it. Yet he was strangely dissatisfied.

Later he wrote, "I began like Alexander of old to feel a strange emptiness—'No more worlds to conquer.' " In the early part of 1940 Wendell Willkie, who was to be the Republican Presidential candidate that year, had sent for Adam. "I went to his office in New York City. We were closeted alone. He pointed out his dreams and his hopes and he almost won me to his cause. These are the Willkie words that scared me: 'Powell, I would like you to be part of my team. I would like you to play a major role. I like independents. But whether you join my team or not, Powell, remember this—always keep yourself independent. Don't let any of these political parties control you.' "

Willkie's words struck a responsive chord inside Adam Clayton Powell. He had not seriously thought about entering politics before. After all, Harlem politics were controlled by whites, and not one of the few black elected officials really represented the nearly half-million blacks in New York City. He had a great ambition to advance the cause of black people as well as great ambition for himself, and what better way to nurture both ambitions than to enter politics? In September of 1941, in an announcement that actually surprised few people, he declared his candidacy for New York's City Council. No black man had ever served on the council before, and it was time one did, Adam told the huge crowd assembled at the Golden Gate. He would run as an Independent, refusing to accept the support of either the Republican or the Democratic party. He felt he could win without that support, and he would owe neither party anything.

His campaign slogan was, One people! One fight! One victory! He had very little money, but he did have scores of willing workers, in a ready-made organization of members of the People's Committee, members of the congregation of Abyssinian Baptist Church, and marchers and picketers from the previous years.

"In those days we didn't have automatic mimeograph

Reverend Adam Clayton Powell, Jr.,
pastor of the Abyssinian Baptist Church

machines and all, and many of us would volunteer to do mimeographing on a hand machine—how we cranked that thing! But it was all fun," Hattie Dodson recalls.

The Reverend David Licorish, who has been associate minister of Abyssinian Baptist Church for twenty-eight years, was sought out by Dr. Powell to help Adam in his campaign. Dr. Powell had not liked the idea of Adam's running for the City Council at first. The elder Powell was planning to retire as pastor of Abyssinian shortly, and he felt that his son should devote more time to preaching and less time to politics. But once he realized that Adam's mind was made up, he had thrown all his considerable influence behind the campaign.

"It happened that Adam's voice broke down one night and he had chosen Ben Richardson to help him," Licorish remembers. But the stand-in speaker had not been able to excite the crowd and Licorish insisted he could do better if he was allowed to speak. "And they listened to me. When we returned, Adam asked, 'Who did the talking?' and the others said, 'Adam, Licorish did it.' Adam said, 'From now on Licorish is in charge of the truck when I'm not there.' And that's the way it began, and it was a fine experience—up and down the avenues, east side, west side, all around the town. It was a glorious period of campaigning in Harlem. The people took a new interest in politics; they would be there waiting for us on the sidewalk every time we came to speak. Toward the end of the campaign Adam spoke to a deacon of the church, Deacon

Ridgely Jones, and after that I became associate minister."

It was a long and strenuous campaign, and when the election results were announced it was clear the people of Harlem were completely on Adam Powell's side. Of the ninety-nine candidates for the City Council throughout the city, he received the third highest vote total, and New York's City Council got its first black member.

"After he was elected to the City Council he continued to work hard," Hattie Dodson, who was active in Adam's campaign, recalls. "He was always anxious to do something for our people. He not only tried to help the black, but anybody who really needed his help. In those days there were just as many white people coming to his office, looking for assistance, as there were Negro. He didn't turn anybody away."

Sometimes he helped people personally. Pearl Swangson, who sold the books written by Adam Powell, Sr. in the back of the church for years and later worked for Adam and his second wife, Hazel Scott, recalls, "I've seen him take money out of his pocket and give it to a person in need. A person would walk up and say, 'Adam, I'm broke,' and Adam would give money out of his own pocket. He didn't make things like that known publicly."

"He wasn't a person to give money away foolishly," says Lillian Upshur, who by that time was a loyal political worker for Adam Powell, "but he would see to it that there was a way for you to make money, in other words, to work for it. If someone came and said, 'I want a job,' Adam would make a call and the fellow would get a job."

Adam's constituents loved him, but the other councilmen and many politicians felt differently. "They didn't like Adam personally at all," says Lillian Upshur. "Although he was a hard worker as a councilman, he had a certain way that irritated them, you know, more or less laughing at them. They thought him arrogant and flamboyant, and he got a great kick out of irritating them. He came right out and said he had come to disturb, and of course he gained tremendous support from the people of Harlem. The leaders acknowledged his presence and more or less worked with him, but they didn't get close to him. He was a person that you couldn't get too close to, you didn't really know what he was thinking about."

During the one term he served on the council, Adam pressed for resolutions against discrimination in numerous areas, but the position of city councilman proved to be just one step on the ladder for Adam Clayton Powell, Jr., and perhaps he saw it that way from the first. Lillian Upshur remembers: "He said, 'The place to be is not in the City Council; they haven't any power to do things for the people of the city.'"

When the New York state legislature announced it was considering a reapportionment bill that made Harlem practically a separate U.S. congressional district, Adam held yet another mass meeting to declare his candidacy for U.S. Representative from that district. It was only eighteen months after he had been elected to the council, and the reapportionment bill had not even been passed yet. Some felt he had spoken too soon. But the bill was passed, as Adam had predicted, and he was a candidate for Congress.

IV

Adam Clayton Powell, for all his public flamboyance, was a thoughtful man. The decision to run for Harlem's first congressional seat, to try to become the first black congressman from New York, was a major one, and he had given much thought to it.

According to Lillian Upshur, others had first approached him with the idea, and he had sought the advice of still others. "A group of politicians got together and went to Adam and said, 'We want you to be congressman. The first black congressman from New York City.' After that, Adam told me that he went to A. Philip Randolph and assured Randolph that if the older man wished to run for the congressional seat he would step aside and A. Philip

Randolph could be the first congressman." Randolph de-
clined the offer and in 1944, when the first election for the
office of U.S. Representative was held in the new 18th
Congressional District, Adam Powell ran and won, this
time as a Democrat.

In politics Adam was becoming more and more successful; his private life, though, was very unhappy. Isabel had
been against his running for the City Council, and when
he decided to run for Congress she had begged him not to
do so. According to Adam, she was afraid of losing him,
and she clutched at him so tightly that he finally walked
out. They were divorced in 1945.

On December 17, 1944, the walls of the Golden Gate
Ballroom fairly bulged in their effort to contain all the
people who had gathered to send Adam Clayton Powell
off to Congress. For his part, Adam delivered a moving
address in which he promised to work as hard as he could
to use his position as a congressman to help black people.
"In my platform I outlined that I would push for fair racial practices, fight to do away with restrictive covenants
and discrimination in housing, fight for the passage of a
national Fair Employment Practices Commission and for
the abolition of the poll tax, fight to make lynching a
Federal crime, do away with segregated transportation,
undergird the Thirteenth, Fourteenth, and Fifteenth
Amendments to the Constitution, protest the defamation of
any group—Protestant, Catholic, Jew, or Negro—fight
every form of imperialism and colonialism, and support
'all legislation, one hundred per cent, to win the war, to

win the peace, pro-labor and pro-minority.' "

"Congressman Adam Clayton Powell, Jr." What a wonderful sound that phrase had for the people of Harlem, indeed to black people all over the country. To many whites, however, it was a curse. Adam was the fourth black man to be elected to the House of Representatives since the Reconstruction period, and for these whites that was four too many. Adam found this out on his way to Washington in January, 1945.

"Adam used to tell us some funny little anecdotes, things that happened when he first went to Congress, when you traveled by train," Gwen Jones recalls. "He told us one time about a man who talked to him all the way down to Washington. He said he'd heard about this colored man coming down to Washington and about what folks said they were going to do to him, and what he himself was going to do to him. There was a lot of this kind of talk, I gather. Adam said he talked all the way down and it never occurred to him to ask who Adam was. As they were leaving the train the man said 'Oh, by the way, what's your name?' and Adam said, 'Adam Powell.' He knew how to handle people like that."

Almost as soon as he had taken his seat in the House, the Speaker of the House, Sam Rayburn of Texas, approached Congressman Powell with some words of caution. "Adam," Rayburn said, "everybody down here expects you to come with a bomb in both hands. Now don't do that, Adam. Oh, I know all about you and I know that you can't be quiet very long, but don't throw those bombs. Just see how things operate here. Take your time. Freshmen members of Congress are supposed not to be heard and not even to be seen too much. There are a lot of good men around here. Listen to what they have to say, drink it all in, get reelected a few more times, and then start moving. But for God's sake, Adam, don't throw those bombs."

Adam's answer was brief: "Mr. Speaker, I've got a bomb in each hand, and I'm going to throw them right away." With that exchange, the two men began a close friendship that lasted until Rayburn's death many years later.

Washington, D.C., was a segregated city in 1945. There were Jim Crow streetcars and railroad cars, segregated restaurants, job discrimination of various kinds, and this discrimination extended right up to the Capitol, the symbol of democracy. When Adam Powell arrived he found a host of unofficial rules that black congressmen were supposed to follow: he was not supposed to use the congressional dining room or gymnasium or barbershop, or to invite black journalists to sit in the congressional galleries. The few other black congressmen before him, including William L. Dawson who was currently a member of the House, had abided by these rules, but not Adam Powell. Before he got down to the business of legislating, he attended to the business of this unofficial discrimination.

Hattie Dodson, who went to Washington with Adam to be his secretary, remembers when black representatives

Representative Adam Clayton Powell, Jr.,
with Representative William Dawson of Chicago

from groups across the country arrived in Washington to urge the establishment of a Fair Employment Practices Commission. This commission would be a watchdog agency, overseeing and checking upon the hiring practices of all industries in the United States. If a company refused to hire or to promote a worker or to pay him fairly because of race, color, or creed, that worker would be able to take his case to the Fair Employment Practices Commission. It was ironic that these delegates who were in Washington to push for a commission against discrimination should be worried about discrimination themselves.

"Adam met with the delegates in his offices," Hattie Dodson recalls, "and then he asked how many would like to have lunch with him in the Capitol dining room. Of course it was unusual for a group of blacks to go to the Capitol dining room. About twenty-five decided they would like to have lunch with him. He said to me, 'Call down and make arrangements for luncheon.' When I called down, the hostess said we would have to have one congressman at each table. The tables seated five people, and one of them had to be a congressman, so we had to line up five other congressmen in order to take care of the seating. Adam said, 'That's all right.' So we got busy and called five other congressmen. Vito Marcantonio was one of them—he was quite liberal, quite vocal, a great help. I don't remember if William Dawson was invited or not; I don't remember any of the other congressmen. As far as I can remember, they were all white.

"The other secretary, Miss Nelson, and I stayed up in the office, and when we didn't hear anything we were all nerves. Finally I called down to the restaurant and asked for Mr. Powell. When he came to the phone I said, 'Everything all right?' and he said, 'Fine, fine, fine!' so we were happy. That was the first time."

Lewis Upshur remembers a similar incident involving the congressional dining room that occurred in 1947, just after he married Lillian, Adam's political aide. "Adam sent for me to come down to Washington, saying, 'Bring all the guys you can, I want to show you something.' I got some men together and we went down. When we got there he said, 'I'm going to take you to the congressional restaurant.' I said to him, 'You called me all the way down here for this?' He said, 'I called you down here because they don't have a black man or a black woman in there other than the bus boy.' We went in, and those crackers were staring like mad. Adam said to us in a loud voice, 'Get on line, get on line,' and to the people who were serving he said, 'Look, I'm a congressman, and these are my guests, and I remember everybody's guests have a right to eat in this congressional restaurant.' That's what made all of the black people in Washington love Adam."

Adam made similar assaults upon segregation practiced in the congressional barbershop and gymnasium and, finally, he publicly exposed the use of the word "nigger" by certain Southern congressmen. Until then the House stenographer had always substituted the word Negro, in the record, but by bringing the matter up in the House,

Adam forced the congressmen's actual words to be recorded in the *Congressional Record*. His actions created quite a stir.

Meanwhile, Congressman Powell was being kept very busy in his office in the Rayburn Building, about a twenty-minute walk from the Capitol Building. Every congressman expects mail from the people in his district, but Adam Powell's constituents were all the black people in the country. "Millions of Negro people in the South had no congressman to speak for them," he later wrote. "They were the disenfranchised, the ostracized, the exploited, and when they pressed upon me their many problems of many years, I could not refuse them because I love all people. Then there were the problems of the people of the District of Columbia, with a population that was then close to being half Negro. They too had no vote and no one to speak for them."

Every day countless letters and phone calls came in, and Adam's poor Washington staff was hard-put to deal with all of them. And there was much more work besides the cases of people who appealed to Powell for help; there was all the work involved in preparing the legislation that he introduced. Sometimes there just didn't seem to be enough hours in the day.

Hattie Dodson recalls, "He was a perfectionist when it came to work. He would give you work to do and leave you. When he'd come back he'd expect it to be done. I can't say he was hard, but you were supposed to deliver. And then sometimes when everybody would be working hard, in the midst of everything he would stop and tell a joke, to relax everybody."

One thing Adam learned soon after being seated in Congress was that you had to keep your sense of humor; you couldn't take yourself too seriously. Like all freshman congressmen, he worked hard on his first speech, and it came as a shock to learn that hardly anyone cared to hear it. "You stand there with a document on which you have labored and you look around and no one is there to hear you except two or three members of the press. . . . So when you read about an important speech on foreign policy or some other earth-shaking matter of grave concern to the nation, frequently no one has heard it. Oftimes it is not even delivered. Under the rules of Congress . . . one needs only to read two or three words of his opening remarks and can insert the rest into the *Congressional Record* as if the full text had actually been delivered orally."

Very little of a congressman's time was actually spent in the House of Representatives. A great deal was wasted on meaningless speeches, calls for votes on minor issues, arguments over matters of procedure. It did not take Adam long to learn that bills were passed or defeated only formally on the floor of the House; the real work was done behind the scenes, in the halls of the Capitol, over lunch in some nearby restaurant, in smoke-filled congressional offices. Adam wasted little time in learning the ways of Washington and plunged into the business of congressional politicking immediately. Freshmen congressmen were traditionally expected to keep quiet, listen, and learn for their first term. Not Adam Powell. He was the sole voice for black Americans; he could waste no time.

In his first term he introduced bills calling for the abolishment of lynching and the poll tax, and for the elimination of segregation in the armed forces and many other areas of American society. They were bills that would help not only the people of the 18th Congressional District in Harlem but also the black people in the rest of the country.

The bill for which Adam worked the hardest during his first years in Congress was for the establishment of a Fair Employment Practices Commission. Such a commission had been authorized by the state legislature of New York just before Adam had arrived in Washington as a new congressman, and his bill, which he introduced almost as soon as he arrived, was copied almost word for word from the New York legislation. Immediately, influential men in both parties publicly announced their support for the bill, but influential support or not the bill had to go into committee first. Adam's bill went into the House Education and Labor Committee, where it stayed for four years. In 1950 Graham Barden, the chairman of the committee, a man who agreed with the bill and wished to see it passed, created a Special Subcommittee on the FEPC and appointed Adam with full power as its chairman. Adam was free to select his committee and, in what seemed a shrewd move, he chose as one of the members a young uncompromising anti-Communist named Richard Nixon. The bill was encountering criticism as Communist-inspired and Adam sought to blunt this criticism by having a strong anti-Communist on his committee. In the end, Richard Nixon voted against the bill in subcommittee and when finally the bill reached the floor of the House for a vote, it was defeated. In its place was passed a weak substitute which gave the FEPC fewer powers than Adam's bill proposed. Adam called it "toothless." More than anything else, he wished he could be chairman of the House Education and Labor Committee, so that he could get some bills passed.

For Adam the defeat of his FEPC bill was a great blow, but he had some important successes during those years. One such success involved the United Nations, which in the mid-1940s was a very possible dream, but not yet a reality. Much planning needed to be done, and a United Nations conference was to be held to make these plans. Adam demanded that a black sit at this first conference, pointing out that this would mean a great deal to the peoples of Asia and Africa who had not yet gained their independence and thus would not be represented at the conference. That such blacks as Marian Anderson, Ralph Bunche, and Zelma George would later serve as members of the United States delegation to the United Nations was due in no small measure to Adam Powell's initial demands for black representation.

Another first for Adam was insuring that a black graduated from the United States Naval Academy at Annapolis, Maryland. Each congressman is allowed to appoint five young men to Annapolis and four to West Point, the United States Military Academy. As a few blacks had graduated from West Point, Adam chose Annapolis as his target, appointing Wesley Brown, a bright young black man from Washington. But Adam realized just getting a black into Annapolis would not assure his graduation, so Adam took steps to make sure nothing happened to Wesley Brown along the way.

A few months after the young man entered Annapolis, Adam wrote a letter to James V. Forrestal, Secretary of the Navy, complaining that Wesley Brown was in danger of being driven out of Annapolis by hostile forces. Forrestal immediately paid a visit to Annapolis to find out what was happening, but to his puzzlement he could find nothing wrong. "This I knew," Adam later wrote. "I had deliberately fabricated that letter in order to make sure nothing would happen to Wesley Brown. . . . And so Wesley was the first black man to be graduated from Annapolis and he has gone on to become a career man in the United States Navy."

It seemed to Adam that everywhere he looked he saw something that needed changing, some injustice that had to be stopped. In January of 1947 he introduced a bill to give the citizens of Washington, D.C., the right to vote, and on the same day he began his campaign to allow black newsmen access to the House Gallery. Suddenly noticing that every face in the press section was white, he asked who was in charge of seating there. He found that it was the members of the press themselves and that the white reporters did not want blacks admitted. Adam went to his friend Speaker Sam Rayburn, and on March 19th the first black face appeared in the press gallery.

There was so much to do. Adam needed a much larger staff than he had to examine all the bills that were introduced, for each one needed careful consideration. In those years before civil rights legislation, there were no federal safeguards against segregation. No provision was made to deny federal monies to states or institutions that practiced segregation. Early in his congressional career, Adam realized that it was up to him to see that such clauses were added. Was there some amendment that could be phrased in simple words which through the years might serve as a point upon which the isolated, backward, and reactionary thinking of men could be turned? Adam asked himself. He sat down, pencil in hand, and thought, and the words came to him: "No funds under this Act shall be made available to or paid to any State or school . . ."

Adam's first chance to introduce this amendment came in 1946. Congress had passed a law providing free school lunches to school children. Under his amendment, no school district that practiced segregation would be eligible for monies under the federal school lunch program. It was passed and became a law on June 4, 1946. Adam Clayton Powell had been responsible for the first piece of civil rights legislation ever passed.

In the following years Adam would introduce that amendment—which came to be called the Powell Amendment—and see it passed many more times, especially when the bills in question affected schools and children. Not until 1954 did the Federal Government relieve him of some of the burden of trying to prevent federal monies from going to segregated schools. In that year the Supreme Court declared "separate but equal" schools unconstitutional, and integrated schools became law.

Most black people loved Adam Powell; he told Mr. Charley where it was at, and he didn't take any back talk. Whites, most of them anyway, didn't like him at all. He was too uppity; in fact, he was a real threat to many whites. "I can see why white people hated Adam," Lewis Upshur says. "Boy, Adam would really strut. We'd be walking down the corridor and we would pass a big chairman of some committee and Adam wouldn't speak to him, just keep walking, talking to me or somebody else. Then he'd go down in the elevator and enter the subway and start to kid with the guys on the subway. To the cleaning woman he'd say, 'Hello, baby; hello, baby'; to the congressman he wouldn't open his mouth."

"He always sympathized with the underdog. I think that was more true of him than of his father," adds Adam's brother-in-law, C. D. King. "Matter of fact, he was criticized for that, but he never did try to hang out with the people who were in his class. Most of his friends were people who were in a lower spot. I never heard him try to explain it, but I heard him speak of stuffed shirts and expressions of that kind about people who thought themselves better than the common people."

"Adam didn't go around with so-called society," says Lewis Upshur. "He said to me many times, 'I've got to go to this in Washington, but I'm either going early before anybody gets there or late after everybody leaves.' "

At first he had been invited to public and private parties out of politeness and curiosity, and as a congressman he received invitations to presidential receptions. His unconcealed dislike for these gatherings, combined with his public statements against the Congress and against individual congressmen, soon made him unpopular in Washington social circles. When he called President Harry S Truman "that little man in the White House," his name began to be dropped from the Presidential reception lists. Adam had little respect for Truman. When the Daughters of the American Revolution, who owned Washington, D.C.'s only large concert hall, refused to allow Hazel Scott and other black performers to appear there, Truman's commissioners upheld the DAR's segregationist policy. Under Truman, no Negro was employed at the White House except as a messenger or a janitor. As far as Adam Powell was concerned, Truman was a "little man," and Adam Powell always said what he thought.

Why did Adam make a point of irritating people? It certainly did not help his position in Congress. But perhaps it was a way to get back at the Hill for all the bitter frustrations he encountered there. Hattie Dodson says, "I remember many times Mr. Powell would come out of a committee meeting, and some of those segregationists had been there, and they would have stymied progress on some bill. You'd have a bill and the chairman of the committee would keep it—you've heard it said they could put it in their pocket?—well they could, and it would never come out before the committee. He would come in very upset, his face very red. I'd ask, 'What's the matter?' and he'd say, 'Honey, they don't mind calling you nigger right to your face.' He had to take a lot when he went down there —just like the other blacks who have blazed the trail. Like ballplayers, they had to take it. And Adam had to take the deepest hurts."

Sometimes Adam would remark that the only thing that kept him going was his knowledge that the people of Harlem were behind him all the way. Reverend Adam Clayton Powell, Sr. had retired as pastor of Abyssinian Baptist Church in 1937 and Adam had been named his successor, and thus he was not only a congressman but the minister of the largest black congregation in America. Although he relied upon Reverend David Licorish and other trusted aides, he returned nearly every Sunday to preach a sermon at Abyssinian Baptist Church, drawing thousands to his services.

"He never lost his ties with the church," says Gwen Jones, who was in charge of Abyssinian's Youth Center in those years. "I probably never was as close to the political scene as some of the others who worked with him, but after a while it got so his political life and his church life were pretty closely meshed. He referred many of the people who asked him for help to the church, because he felt that we would take care of people. If someone wrote to him in Washington—for some reason he never established a congressional office in the 18th District, his office was always the church—he would refer the problem to several people close to him in New York."

Lillian Upshur says, "He never forgot the people; he'd come back and report at the Golden Gate Ballroom about what was done in Congress, what bills were up, how he had broken the discrimination against blacks that had existed when he first got there."

"He made good use of the mass meeting," Gwen Jones says of the Golden Gate gatherings. "The People's Committee would meet there, and thousands of people would come to hear about national problems. He made Harlem grow away from just community problems and begin to think of the whole spectrum, which is something I've never seen any other congressman do." Adam could see this awakening awareness in the people of Harlem, and it helped when the going got rough in Washington.

But while the going was rough in Washington, Adam's private life was running smoothly once more.

True to the previous pattern, while Adam's political life was filled with problems, his private life was happy. He had fallen in love with another woman, Hazel Scott.

Adam and Hazel had met in the early 1940s and he had been impressed with her immediately. She had already made seven motion pictures and was acknowledged to be one of the best night club entertainers in the country, but these accomplishments were not what impressed Adam. Her personality was one of the most dynamic he had ever known, and though she had never been to college she was extremely intelligent and spoke several languages fluently. As Adam's marriage to Isabel Washington became more and more empty, he began to see

Hazel Scott as often as their busy lives allowed.

After his divorce from Isabel in July of 1945, Adam took Hazel to meet his father. Like Isabel, Hazel was in show business and of a lower social class than the Powells, but Dr. Powell took to her immediately. "Hazel was somebody who had come up by her talent and ability to play the piano and sing—she had lifted herself," C. D. King explains. Dr. Powell and Adam would take Hazel and her mother fishing, and Adam could often be found at Hazel's house in North White Plains, New York. Shortly after he was elected to Congress, Adam asked Hazel to marry him. The marriage took place in August of 1945.

It was a small wedding in a little church in Connecticut, with only three people present. Afterward, they returned to the city for a huge reception at the Café Society, the club where Hazel had been performing when she and Adam had met. Following the reception, they had planned to go to Vermont to a chalet in the mountains which Adam had leased for the summer from the former chief justice of the supreme court in Vermont. The night before the wedding, however, Adam received a call from the justice who explained that his neighbors in Vermont would not have a Negro living in their area. He would stand behind Adam and Hazel, the man assured him, but the situation could become unpleasant. Adam agreed that a honeymoon was no time for unpleasant situations, and he and Hazel honeymooned in a suite in New York's Waldorf Astoria.

For Adam, his and Hazel's marriage was an ideal one. He had thought about why his marriage to Isabel had not

Adam Powell with his second wife,
jazz pianist Hazel Scott

worked and had decided a chief reason was that she had given up her career in show business when they were married. He had grown and she had not, and he felt that she had tried to hold him back. Hazel had not given up her career; in fact, just one month after their marriage she left on her first transcontinental tour. Adam felt that they could share a life together and at the same time pursue their individual careers, growing together, each making a contribution.

To those who were close to them, their relationship seemed perfect. "They spoke the same language," says Pearl Swangson who, as Hazel's secretary–hairdresser, lived and traveled with them for several years. "She was good in history and music, and he never wrote his speeches without asking her advice—it was the same with his sermons. And Hazel would often ask his advice; she would say, 'Well, Adam, if it's all right with you I will say so-and-so.' They were very close." When, in October of 1945, Hazel announced that she was pregnant, Adam was overjoyed; a child would bring them even closer together.

Adam Clayton Powell, III was born on June 17, 1946. Almost from the beginning they called him Skipper, after a boat that they kept out on Long Island. It is fitting that the little boy's nickname was taken from a boat: "One of my earliest memories of my father was when I was two or three—certainly no older than three and a half," recalls Skipper Powell. "We were on a boat off Panama and I was sitting on his lap in one of those deep-sea fishing chairs. He had put me in his lap so I could help him reel in a tuna." Skipper would later become an avid fisherman.

"I was born in Sydenham Hospital," Skipper Powell continues, "and at that time we lived at 130th Street and St. Nicholas Avenue. When I was one or two we moved up to White Plains for six months or so, and then to Mt. Vernon. The house had been built on the line between Mt. Vernon and Bronxville, but it was at the end of a dead-end road that had a woods behind it. It was a remarkable neighborhood, because there seemed to be one of everybody on the block. We were the only Negroes; our neighbors to the south were Jewish; in the next house they were German–Catholic."

Although Adam's and Hazel's careers kept them away a lot, they made great efforts to provide a real home and family life for Skipper. "One of my earliest memories is of coming in from playing—even before I was in school— and asking the maid, 'Who's home tonight?' And she'd say, 'Your father's home,' or 'Your mother's home,' or 'They're both home,' or whatever, because my mother was always traveling on concert tours and my father was spending most of his time in Washington. What I didn't know at first was that they had an agreement whereby they would try to arrange their schedules so that one or the other would be in town on any given evening, and that both of them would be in on Saturdays, or at least Saturday morning. This, as you can imagine, took considerable rearranging of their schedules. I got a definite impression from both of them that this was something they felt was very important. I'd sometimes hear my father saying, 'I can't see Eisenhower on Saturday,' so I knew that they were going through special things to schedule those days in New York.

"One of my strongest memories is of the whole weekend routine that evolved. On Saturdays, or late Friday night after I was asleep, they would both be in. Saturday morning we'd always do something together, almost always something outdoors. My father was very big on playing ball—softball or football. There was one part of the yard outside the house in Mt. Vernon that was long and narrow, and for years we played softball, sometimes just the two of us, sometimes with other kids in the neighborhood. Sometimes in the fall my father and my mother used to play football with all the kids on the block and myself. I remember my mother's agent having a fit. He'd say, 'Oh my God, you're going to break a finger! What are you doing?' Saturday night was a pretty set routine— my father would go into his study and start working on his sermons for the next morning, and I'd go and wash the car. I used to love washing his car, a beautiful blue Jaguar.

"We used to go fishing a lot.. We had a place out in Westhampton, Long Island, in the summer, and my mother was always amazed at us. The two of us would go out and sit behind the house and fish for flounder all day. She'd exclaim, 'How the two of you can go out and sit there all day, in the rain, with little glass rods, waiting for one of those fish!' The next house down was this little pink house, and all I knew was that a nice man lived in the pink house. It wasn't until I was about sixteen that I realized the nice man named Charles Addams who lived in the pink house was the same Charles Addams who did the cartoons in *The New Yorker* magazine."

Famous people were just people to young Skipper Powell. "They used to give very large parties in the big living room, and I can remember having to go to bed very early, with the party still going on downstairs and people playing the piano or whatever. I remember shocking a man whom I had never met before when I repeated one of those phrases that parents use but children aren't supposed to repeat. I was about four at the time and I was going upstairs and my father was saying, 'Well, it's time to go to bed,' and I said, 'Yes, if I don't go to bed I'll get bags under my eyes like Duke Ellington has.' Of course you know who was sitting right there! I saw Duke Ellington about a year or two ago, and he looked at me and said, 'Well, I see you have been getting enough sleep.' "

Trips to Europe were nearly as common as fishing trips. "On my first trip I went with both of them; it was 1949, so I would have been three. We stayed in London; we had an apartment in a fairly high building because I can remember going up the steps. We were there about four or five months. My mother would sometimes go off for a day or two to play in Glasgow or someplace. We went in the summer when Congress was out of session and stayed through December. My father went back for the beginning of Congress, and I went back having missed the first half of prekindergarten.

"We went every summer for a while, and I could never keep the trips separate in my mind except for a few things. I remember in 1955 we went to Berchtesgaden and we went trout fishing. There was a trout that my father was determined to get—an almost legendary trout that would be a world record if it could be caught. It lived in a little pool off a fast-moving stream, which I was always falling into, and there were bushes hanging over it. People would try to cast under those bushes and they'd always get tangled up or they'd miss altogether. One day, for some reason, he got the hang of casting into that little pool and he just kept casting and casting. Finally, in water so clear and beautiful that you could see this trout lying under there, the trout went for the bait. My father started reeling —this was an incredible feat because the line wasn't tested for that large a fish. It was getting closer and closer. There was somebody from the Air Force there and people from Berchtesgaden stumbling into the water, trying to get a look at this incredible fish. He maneuvered the fish to the boat and brought it up, and people were just gasping. The Air Force officer brought up a net under him. And do you know, that fish got out of the net and broke the line! My father's first words were, 'Where's he going, where's he going?' "

Adam Powell and Hazel Scott with their son,
Adam Clayton Powell III

Skipper Powell was the first black to go to the private Riverdale Academy. "Hazel gave a concert at Riverdale when she was carrying Skipper," Pearl Swangson explains, "and she gave all the proceeds to the music department. They said, 'Your baby will be the first black student at the school,' and it happened to be a boy, and so Skipper was the first to go there."

"I was bored in school," Skipper recalls. "My paternal grandmother had taught me reading and arithmetic before I went to kindergarten, so when I arrived I was already at about the second grade level. My father was always a big proponent of education. He didn't really push me, but he was always encouraging me to educate myself, which was maddening at times. Sometimes he just wouldn't give me the answer to something, saying, 'Well, you know all the books we have in the study; you can go find it yourself.' I'd say, 'But I know you know!'

"He was not really stern, but gently demanding. I remember once in fourth grade I'd gotten all A's. But they had another mark for effort, on a scale of 1 for the most effort to 5 for the worst. All my marks were A–4, A–5, A–4, A–5. He didn't say, 'That's terrible. Why aren't you doing more work?' But he did say something like, 'You know, we really should try to put more effort into something as worthwhile as school.' He was always indirect, but in a direct way."

Skipper Powell had a surprisingly normal childhood, considering that his parents were two extraordinary people. "The first hint I remember that there was anything extraordinary in the way I was living came one night when I was allowed to stay up until 11:00. All I knew was that my father had been out of town—he'd gone someplace for a week or so—and that my mother was very excited. I was about nine, and I remember it was in the middle of the week, a school day, and John K. M. McCaffery was doing the 11:00 news. He would always say, 'What kind of day has it been?' and the first item was, 'Adam Clayton Powell is leaving Bandung tonight, after having . . .' I said, 'Oh, what do you know, my father's on television.' After that I would always ask him, 'What are you doing now? What have you done lately?' and he'd say, 'Well, in Washington we've done this and that. . . .' "

VI

In Washington Adam Clayton Powell had been doing as much as he could, although he would have liked to do a great deal more. Getting bills passed in Congress depends on a number of factors, but the two chief ones are that you must have allies and you must have power. Adam Powell was not very well-liked in Washington. Some disliked him because he was a Negro, others disliked his flamboyance and his habit of "dropping bombs," others criticized his frequent trips to Europe and frequent absences from the floor of the House. Adam knew he couldn't do anything about those who disliked him for personal reasons, but to the charge of absence he insisted he was always there when something important was being considered or voted upon.

He explained his feelings in his autobiography: "In the majority of cases the many quorum calls that abruptly summon one across Independence Avenue to answer on the floor are instituted by the whims and caprices of a single member. . . . There are men in Congress who have never contributed anything to the advancement of our nation, but sit all day on the floor of Congress, just to look around and see whether two hundred and eighteen members are present. If not, they question the presence of quorum. Then the Speaker makes a count, finds there is no quorum, and three bells are rung. One must then scurry over to answer the roll call. This I refused to do. . . . When there is a roll call it takes twenty-two minutes to go from an office in the Rayburn Building, where my office was; and voting and coming back would consume—unless one has a car and a chauffeur ready—almost an hour. . . . Thus I always picked only those votes that were important. Proof of this is that the AFL–CIO always rated me as one of the best congressmen on voting, as did the NAACP and the ADA."

The people of the 18th Congressional District in Harlem didn't seem to have any complaints about their congressman; every two years they sent him back to Congress by a huge vote margin. It got so he didn't even have to campaign.

"His real power base was the poor underdog," says Lewis Upshur, who helped direct Adam's re-election bids every two years, "and he knew it. Once he was campaigning at 148th Street and Eighth Avenue, and some guy started heckling him. 'Congressman Powell,' he said, 'I got some wine over here. Why don't you come over?' Adam said, 'You stay there until I finish speaking, then you and I will go around the corner and have a drink.' So the guy stayed, and when Adam was finished he walked around the corner and had a drink. Everybody was happy about it because he was with the people of the street."

Even so, in the 1940s and early 1950s, a man could have had every black in America behind him and still have little power in Congress. Black people were unorganized, many could not even vote—and it takes organization and voting strength to wield political clout.

In Congress it is the chairmen of committees who have the real power, and in order to be a chairman you must have been in Congress for a very long time, longer than Adam Clayton Powell had. Major bills were always the result of the work of these committees.

"He was often frustrated," Skipper Powell recalls. "There was nothing he could do but attack amendments on the floor. At one point he was given a subcommittee on the Interior—he was in charge of mines and mining—and he held some fascinating hearings on mine safety. He would talk about conditions in the mines: 'It's really horrible, maybe I'll write a book on it.' I'd ask, 'Why don't you draft a law on mine safety?' and he'd say, 'Oh, we'd never get it through.' Then he'd draw an imaginary picture of the House of Representatives for me and go through the chambers area by area. 'First of all, write off the Republicans —they're not going to vote for it. You can get some of them, maybe, but it'll take some really strong trading. Then you have to write off a whole section of this aisle, and then a section of that aisle. You're left with maybe eighty or ninety votes you can count on, and maybe you can get your total up to a hundred and fifty, but that's not enough to get the bill through.' "

In November, 1952, Dwight David Eisenhower, the most celebrated general in World War II, outpolled Democrat Adlai Stevenson to be elected to the Presidency. His Vice-President was Richard M. Nixon. Adam Powell groaned publicly. As he wrote in his autobiography, "I pondered whether it was worthwhile to continue the fight. We now had a man in the White House who refused to open his mouth to say one word concerning civil rights while our nation was being shamed throughout the world. And we had as Vice-President Richard Nixon. . . . With these two in the White House, I felt at first there was little hope for Negro legislative progress, and I ceased introducing bills of a civil rights nature. Then that same still voice came to me and said, 'Do not give up. Maybe their high positions will make these men into the kind of human beings they should be.' "

During that first Eisenhower term it seemed to Adam that his faith had been rewarded. The President appointed an unprecedented forty-seven blacks to important posts, eliminated segregation in Southern naval bases and installations and in Veterans Administration hospitals. One of the most significant changes made during those first Eisenhower years was the desegregation of Washington,

D.C., a change that was due in no small measure to Adam Clayton Powell. Eisenhower had publicly stated that he favored desegregation of the capital and had instructed the Board of Commissioners of the District of Columbia, whom he had appointed, to move against all forms of discrimination there. But Adam learned in the early months of the Administration that the Secretary of Health, Education, and Welfare, Mrs. Oveta Culp Hobby, planned deliberately to disobey the President's instructions. Immediately Adam drafted a telegram to Eisenhower, informing him of the plan and demanding that he assert his integrity by making sure his instructions were indeed followed. Shrewdly, Adam saw to it that a copy of the telegram reached the offices of the Washington *Evening Star* that very day, June 3, 1953.

Adam later wrote, "No single event caused more disturbance in the White House than when President Eisenhower read the headlines that night in the Washington *Evening Star*. He instructed Max Rabb to call a special Cabinet meeting. Max Rabb came running to my office to complain. 'Adam, you have made a great mistake. Things are in an uproar in the White House. Why didn't you get in touch with me first?'

" 'Max, maybe I did make a mistake in the manner in which I handled this, but I am sick and tired of the White House under every administration saying one thing and the people who work under the White House doing the opposite.'

" 'Well, Adam, I tell you what to do: the President is going to write you a letter and I want you to reply in a complimentary way, and from here on we walk together. We have received orders to do everything within reason to wipe out segregation and discrimination in the Federal Government.' "

Within a matter of months, all restaurants, bars, and hotels in the city were desegregated, as were theaters and recreational areas. It was all done so quietly that some blacks didn't even know about it until, to their astonishment, they were allowed entrance into a previously segregated restaurant or were sold tickets at a previously segregated theater.

The greatest event for black Americans that occurred during that first Eisenhower Administration was the 1954 Supreme Court decision that declared "separate but equal" schools unconstitutional. Not only was it a landmark decision of itself but also it marked the real beginning of the civil rights movement in America.

Other black leaders emerged, notably Dr. Martin Luther King, Jr., and for the first time since becoming a national figure Adam Powell was not the only black man speaking out strongly for the rights of black people in America. That is not to say that he stopped speaking out for black Americans, but now he had more time to consider the problems of other nonwhite peoples.

The conference of newly independent Asian and African nations in Bandung, Indonesia, in 1955 in many ways represented a turning point in Adam's life. Prior to the Bandung Conference he was a nationalist; after it he became an internationalist.

The conference, on April 19, 1955, was an extraordinary event, for it was the first time in history that nations of Asia and Africa (twenty-nine in all) met to discuss the problems of newly independent non-white countries. The United States was against the conference, and when Adam decided to attend at his own expense, everything possible was done to dissuade him.

"Why did the Department of State not want an American to go to what has now become the most important conference in modern times?" Adam later wrote. "Simply because we did not have an adequate foreign policy for Asia and Africa. . . . We have too many leaders in our nation who are color-blind, who see only white. Three-fifths of the free peoples of the world are colored, and this means that the United States is in danger of becoming a second-class power by letting history pass it by."

Adam was firm in his intention to attend the Bandung Conference, and although the government did everything from pleading with him to reconsider to offering him attractive, but officially directed missions to Asia and Africa, he refused to change his mind. On March 29, 1955, he addressed the Congress before leaving for Bandung, Indonesia, explaining that he felt there should be a member of the United States Government there to show that the country was sympathetic to the aims for peace of the nations attending the conference.

"At the conclusion of my speech," he later recalled, "members of Congress—Northerners, Southerners, Republicans, and Democrats—rose to their feet, praised me, and wished me Godspeed. Then, and only then, did the Department of State offer to give me some assistance, and the only reason was, and I quote their representative, 'If we do not give you complete cooperation and if our embassy ignores you while you are there, then the Communists will say that we are doing this to you because you represent a minority.' " Even so, Adam carried no message of good will from President Eisenhower when he arrived at Bandung.

Adam had feared that the Communist countries of Russia and Red China would use the United States' refusal to participate in the conference to their own advantage, and he was correct. These two countries planned to attract as many of the new Asian and African nations as possible to communism and to turn them away from democracy. Their main argument would be racism—if the United States treats its own minorities so poorly how do you expect the United States to treat you? This was why Adam had so strongly urged United States participation, and one reason why he attended the conference despite tremendous pressure against his going. In the sort of public performance for which he had become well known in the United States, Adam made sure that no question of racism in the United States came up.

He called a press conference prior to the start of the meeting, and to the hundreds of reporters, including every

*Representative Powell at the Afro-Asia
Conference, Bandung, Indonesia*

representative of the Communist press, who came to hear him, he insisted that black Americans had made many gains. He urged the attending nations to consider the question from all sides and not to believe the Communists without question. At home in the United States, the Hearst newspapers reported: "At a press conference Adam Powell shot straight from the shoulder at Communist correspondents who tried to trot out the Red charge that the Negro is horribly treated in America. With the oratory for which he is noted, Powell told them that it just isn't so. He said racism and second-class citizenship are on their way out in the United States and pointed pridefully to the number of Negroes who are holding public office."

Adam later wrote in his autobiography: "The final communiqué of the Asian–African conference was definitely pro-West, pro-American, pro-democracy, and pro-United Nations. The United Nations was referred to eighteen times in one way or another as a basis upon which to shape the future of the Asian and African nations and of the world. The communiqué praised the contributions of the United States to their countries. Because of the unanimity rule, Red China had to sign the communiqué, which meant that it joined in praising the United States."

Adam Clayton Powell, the brash *enfant terrible* of Congress, the troublemaker, the black who did not know his place, had singlehandedly helped to combat the Communist influence over the emerging Asian and African nations. Adam returned from Bandung to a hero's welcome. Praise poured in from the press, from United States diplomats, from individual politicians. The House of Representatives passed a resolution commending him for "statesmanship, patriotism, and forthright courage."

"I remember when he came back," Skipper Powell says, "there was tremendous commotion, everybody coming by to talk to him, and he was flying off to see Eisenhower. Then I remember he almost literally locked himself into one of the bedrooms in the house in Mt. Vernon for about two or three weeks, dictating notes to turn into a book on Bandung." Unfortunately, the book was never written.

Adam had recognized the importance of Bandung and had boldly seen to it that the United States participated in the historic moment in spite of itself. But Adam realized that he could do only so much. As he later wrote, "Bandung was a punctuation mark in history. Whether it will be a period, comma, colon, exclamation mark, or question mark depends upon the United States of America."

Meanwhile, another turning point was occurring in the life of Adam Clayton Powell. The marriage which eight years before he had thought could be so perfect was falling apart. It wasn't that he and Hazel were fighting; they just suddenly realized they were drifting away from each other. Hazel had fallen in love with Paris and spent more and more time there. Although she had tried to help Adam in the church, she resented the people of the church, feeling that they stood between herself and her husband. For his part, although he tried to help Hazel with her career,

Adam was jealous of the time and love she gave it. Together they realized that although they loved each other deeply they loved their individual lives more.

"My mother went to live in Paris in 1954," says Skipper Powell, "so I saw my father most of the time from 1954 to 1958. The arrangement was that I would spend the summers in Paris. Between 1958 and 1960 I lived in Paris with my mother and went to school there. After 1960, when I came back from the two years in Paris, I would spend Christmas vacation with her and also some time in June, but I was working most summers.

"Spring vacation I would almost always spend with my father in Washington. They had fairly intricate arrangements. They got along fine and they never had anything but the most complimentary things to say about each other to me. I remember before they broke up they would be saying nice things about each other and I'd be saying, 'That's wonderful. If you think so much of each other, why are you getting divorced?' " But in 1956 Hazel and Adam were divorced.

Once again Adam had lost a wife, and he missed Hazel very much. But he still had his son, and Skipper's memories of that period are fond ones. Adam used to take him along on official trips, such as those to Panama where he was investigating work conditions of white and black workers. When reporters asked how he could explain taking his young son along at the Government's expense, Adam answered, "He's my secretary," and in a way that was the truth.

"I was fascinated by electric typewriters," Skipper Powell recalls, "even as far back as 1953 when I was six or seven or so. I was learning how to type with ten fingers, and I couldn't reach all the keys, so I learned to type with two fingers, and I would address envelopes and type letters and things.

"He had a small house in Washington. We both did the cooking. He loved to cook, and I remember he was delighted one morning when I was five or six years old, I surprised him by making an omelette and bacon. Our tastes were always similar. He loved green vegetables, and one of our favorite meals was hamburger and spinach—it made me very unpopular at school, liking spinach. He also liked to make greens—very, very spicy and hot. Actually he did most of the cooking in Washington; he used to make rather remarkable chile, again very hot. He wouldn't have a huge spice rack, but he'd throw in a lot of things like pigs' feet, and drippings. We had a good time together in Washington."

Although his son was a stable influence, Adam's life in the years between 1954 and 1960 was unsettled and not very satisfying. He was busy, yet he did not feel that he was accomplishing very much, and he was constantly beset with minor, but troublesome irritations.

After the divorce from Hazel he seemed to lack roots, and those close to him could see that he was having a hard time getting over Hazel. "He was moody," recalls Lillian Upshur, who as the leader of his political club in Harlem, the Alfred Isaacs Democratic Club, was in constant touch with him. "He had been deeply hurt, but he wouldn't show it. He would act as flamboyant as ever, and you would never really know what he was feeling.

"After the divorce," Mrs. Upshur continues, "they gave up the house in Fleetwood and Adam didn't have any home in New York. He preferred a room here, a room there, and he didn't spend much time in any of them. He didn't have any servants, except a cleaning woman to do his rooms. He didn't have a valet, but he was very careful with his clothing. He wouldn't go without shining his shoes. A man on 135th Street volunteered to do it free because he was proud of Adam, so from then on Adam sent his shoes over to him."

Harlem did not give him the solace he sought in those years, and he often became impatient with the people at Abyssinian. Sometimes they seemed so petty and blind. He had tried to educate them politically, to make them see the importance of unity within the black community, but there was periodically recurring trouble between the native American blacks and the West Indian blacks in the congregation. This was true of the larger community as well, where the achievement orientation, the desire to get ahead among West Indians was resented by native American blacks. Adam continually preached against such division. Then, too, there were elements in the church who were against Adam, partly out of jealousy, partly out of conservatism that disapproved of his flamboyance and his private life, which was considered not entirely respectable.

"At one time," recalls Reverend David Licorish, "when he had had some trouble with one of his wives—I don't know whether it was before he married Hazel or after—there was a lot of unnecessary gossip. He rose up and invited the troublemakers to leave, and he brought out into the open the fact that they didn't like me because I was West Indian, because I wouldn't join with them, because I was loyal to him. That's the time when we could have walked out of the church and started a new movement. Years later he said to me, 'Lic, we should have split Abyssinian when we had a chance to.' He knew all along that it wasn't the ideal church that he wanted it to be."

As a congressman, Adam was active and outspoken, yet he continued to feel frustrated at his lack of power to push through legislation that would really benefit black people. Attacking segregation in the National Guard and in airports, attaching the Powell Amendment to bills whenever possible—these and other battles for civil rights earned him the reputation of being, as a 1956 *New York Times* editorial put it, "the country's most vocal crusader for Negro rights." The *Times* continued. "He averages a telegram to President Eisenhower every week or two. On the floor of Congress, in articles, statements and numerous public speeches, he denounces public segregation in all its works. His language seldom is mild. . . . Mr. Powell is not a partisan Democrat on the question of Negro rights."

Adam was a partisan of civil rights for black people, and he would support anyone, black or white, Republican or Democrat, who seemed to share the same goal. Nineteen fifty-six was a Presidential election year, and it was in that year that Adam showed just how great a professional risk he was willing to take in the name of Negro rights. He, a Democrat, supported the re-election campaign of Republican President Eisenhower against Democrat Adlai Stevenson.

The 1956 campaign was a rematch between the two candidates who had run in 1952—Eisenhower and Stevenson. In 1952 Adam had supported Stevenson without qualms, for Stevenson's stand on civil rights had been strong and forthright. By 1956, however, Stevenson's civil rights platform had become considerably weakened. Perhaps he felt his liberal stand on civil rights had caused him to lose the 1952 election, and he did not want to make the same mistake again. Whatever his reasons, he was definitely playing down the civil rights amendment that Adam and other liberal Democrats wanted to see included in the Democratic platform. And Stevenson and other party leaders avoided talking with Adam Powell about it.

"They didn't consult him on anything," charges Lillian Upshur. "Adlai Stevenson wanted to come to Harlem to get support, but who did he come to see—Hulan Jack. That's what really made Adam angry. He said, 'They're going to talk to Hulan Jack and not come to me? I'm the congressman; he's just the district leader, an assemblyman!' And Adam went to Illinois and found out that Stevenson had treated the black people worse than any other governor of Illinois. In the election, Stevenson lost the state of Illinois—his own state."

In all conscience, Adam could not support Stevenson, and though it meant bolting the Democratic party, he supported Eisenhower. Many liberal Democrats could not understand his decision: "You'll never get a civil rights bill passed under the Republicans," they warned. Eisenhower was re-elected, and during his second term the 1957 Civil Rights Bill and the 1959 Right-to-Vote Bill were passed.

Although in supporting Eisenhower Adam had reasserted his independence, he paid dearly for doing so. Democrats were determined to get back at him for deserting the party, and Republicans who had disliked him before the election did not feel they owed him anything because he had supported Eisenhower. One month after Eisenhower was re-elected, a grand jury was convened in New York to consider an indictment against Abyssinian Baptist Church for income tax evasion, and all the records of the church for the year 1950, the period during which evasion was charged, were subpoenaed.

Although at this point, income tax evasion was merely charged, not proven, the indictment was sufficient ammunition for those in the House who were against Adam to act. "My two patronage appointments in the House of Representatives were fired by the Democratic leadership," Adam wrote in his autobiography. "My prior claim for a new office was ignored and given to Frank Chelf of Kentucky. And with every single Republican voting against me despite my support of Eisenhower, I was stripped of my seniority on the Committee on Education and Labor. . . . I received only an assignment to an insignificant subcommittee. The seniority of every other member was rigidly respected. Siding with the entire Republican membership were six Northern Democrats."

For a time, it seemed to Adam Powell that all was lost. Stripped of his seniority, the coveted chairmanship of the House Education and Labor Committee appeared forever beyond his reach. And without his seniority on the committee, how could he even hope to push legislation through?

Almost before Adam knew it, the 1958 congressional election was upon him. It would prove to be one of the most difficult he had to fight, for Democrats in New York were out to get him for supporting Eisenhower in 1956. Democratic political bosses in Manhattan had found a man whom they felt had a chance to beat Adam—one Earl Brown—and early in the year they began a vigorous campaign to unseat Adam. The leader of the campaign was Hulan Jack, the Borough President of Manhattan. In the face of such opposition within his own party, Adam decided to run on the Republican ticket. However, he was later persuaded to run in the August Democratic primary and defeated Brown by a large margin. In the general election, therefore, Powell was the candidate of both the Democrats and the Republicans. Earl Brown ran against him on the Liberal ticket.

Not surprisingly, Adam won a resounding victory over Earl Brown in November.

Adam Powell surrounded by supporters
after his victory in the 1958 Democratic primary

The victory was a small beam of light in a period of darkness for Adam, for although he had not been unseated in Congress, it seemed certain that he would be convicted of income tax evasion. The case which the grand jury had convened to consider in early 1957 dragged on. "Not one single agent of the United States Government, the Internal Revenue Service, or the Department of Justice had given me the courtesy extended to criminals, gangsters, and underworld figures—namely, to allow me or my representatives to go over the records for the years in question," Adam wrote. "The chief of the task force set up to go after me . . . testified on the stand under cross-examination by Williams [Adam's lawyer, Edward Bennett Williams] that the procedure in this case was 'not the usual.' When Williams pressed him as to why they had not given the usual treatment to me . . . he said he was acting under orders from the Department of Justice."

Not a single newspaper or magazine except the black publications and the Washington *Evening Star* even tried to be objective. Members of Congress publicly condemned Adam. It seemed, as Adam put it, a "rule-by-mob, get-Powell-damn-the-cost" atmosphere. Adam was probably not entirely innocent of the charges, but as the years went by and the case dragged on, thoughtful individuals were forced to suspect an ulterior motive in the relentless pursuit of Powell. "I ask you if they were conducting an investigation into his taxes, or if they were waging a political vendetta designed to destroy him?" Edward Bennett Williams demanded at one point. And Adam observed ruefully that he was being made to pay for being independent in more ways than one.

Ironically, President Eisenhower, the beneficiary of Adam's act of independence, proved in the end not to be the friend of civil rights that Adam had thought he was. In 1957 black children attempting to attend a previously all-white school in Little Rock, Arkansas, were set upon by a white crowd acting with the support of local police, and their entrance was barred. Federal troops were sent in to see that integration of the school was carried out and peace restored, but this only increased black–white tensions. Adam was in Europe at the time and thus witnessed firsthand the anti-Americanism that the incident stirred abroad. Quickly, he returned to the United States and sent an urgent request to President Eisenhower for a meeting on the Little Rock situation. He was put off.

Four months later, Little Rock was nearly in a state of siege, yet the conference still had not taken place. In a letter to Eisenhower Adam wrote, "Little Rock has not quieted down. Negro churches of God have been destroyed and the perpetrators have gone free. Two murders have taken place within thirty days by law enforcement officers. I can assure you, Mr. President, that if you think a conference is no longer necessary, then you are the recipient of some very bad briefing and advice by your aides. Russia can sweep Asia and Africa on the basis of the dilatory tactics of our Government in the field of equality and time is not on our side." Still, he was put off.

Not until May of 1958 did the President convene a conference of the sort Adam had requested, and ironically he was not invited. Dr. Martin Luther King, Jr. of the SCLC, A. Philip Randolph of the AFL–CIO, Lester Granger of the National Urban League, and Roy Wilkins of the NAACP were invited, but not Adam. Later he would write, "And so, the meeting I had fought to arrange was held without my presence. I could only conclude that the Administration feared that I would take too militant a stand. If so, the fear was justified."

Lillian Upshur recalls, "Adam always said, 'Don't expect anything from anyone that you do something for.' "

As time went on, the tax evasion case against Adam was extended to include not only charges of tax evasion against Abyssinian Baptist Church but against Adam personally and against Hazel, with whom he had filed joint returns during their marriage. The case become so complicated that at times, no end seemed in sight. But finally on April 7, 1960, the end was at hand. All through the case the judge, Frederick Van Pelt Bryan, had retained his objectivity and sense of justice, and on that day he dismissed two of the three counts against Adam. The jury went out to consider the third. After lengthy deliberation, they were unable to agree on a verdict and were dismissed by the judge. The case could have been tried again, but it was dropped by the Government a year later.

"It is impossible to estimate precisely how much the Government spent on this case," Adam reflected later. "Edwin Murray, writing in the New York *Daily News* on March 16, said, 'It is outrageous to think that our

Government would spend $100,000 to prosecute a man like Powell for $3,000. There must be something more than that behind this unwarranted scheme.' " Other members of the press estimated the Government expense at $200,000 to $400,000. The lengths to which the Government had been willing to go to convict him were distressing to Adam. But more important were the questions raised by the case. How in the world can a poor man fight a case in court? And what has happened to the idea that a man is innocent until proven guilty?

Meanwhile, added to his numerous other troubles, Adam was going through a critical period of ill-health. On June 1, 1957, while preaching from the pulpit of Abyssinian Baptist Church, he suffered a heart attack. "High living, too many cigars, and too much liquor," his critics commented, but although Adam did have a fondness for sour mash, his poor health was not so easily explained. In 1947, when he was only thirty-five years old, Adam had suffered two heart attacks in a row, and from then on it seemed he was burdened by ill-health of some sort. In 1959, while he was in the hospital for a hernia operation, doctors discovered a growth on the base of his esophagus that they thought might be cancer. A few weeks later, a part of his esophagus was removed.

"He was born a teacher," Lillian Upshur recalls. "He would use anything as a basis to teach you something. After that operation he came to our house for dinner, and he said, 'I want to show you something. See, they cut me here, they went around here, see that. And they lifted up

*Powell enters Federal Court in New York City, May, 1958,
to plead innocent to charges of income tax evasion.*

this, took out that.' He described everything, gave a lesson on how to operate on an esophagus!" But generally Adam did not like to speak about his health, and those who knew him in those days do not know whether he realized how sick he was; certainly they did not realize.

Although beset by these and other problems during the late 1950s, Adam experienced some happy times, and among the happiest were those in Puerto Rico. After the Bandung Conference and his new interest in other non-white peoples, he had become involved in the affairs of the small United States commonwealth in the Caribbean, and by the late 1950s he was spending much of his time there. Undoubtedly, some of his interest in Puerto Rico was influenced by Mrs. Yvette Marjorie Flores Diago, a young divorcée who went to Washington to work on his staff. Her family was wealthy and very influential in Puerto Rico. In the late 1950s Adam built a house on the island, and in 1960 he married Yvette, hoping once more that he could have a lasting marriage with a woman he loved.

VII

In November, 1960, John F. Kennedy outpolled former Vice-President Richard M. Nixon to become President of the United States, and Adam Clayton Powell saw new hope for black people.

"He and Jack Kennedy were great buddies," recalls Lewis Upshur, who remained a close political aide. With a good friend in the White House, Adam hoped that he would have greater support for the social legislation bills he felt were needed. This hope, however, was tempered by the realization that he was in a poor position to get any of these bills started toward passage. By 1959 Adam had been on the House Education and Labor Committee for fifteen years and was the ranking Majority member. But

Graham Barden of North Carolina, who had been chairman for over ten years, and the other committee members had effectively stripped him of his seniority by denying him the chairmanship of any of the numerous Education and Labor subcommittees. It was a painfully frustrating situation for Adam.

"The last few years, particularly, had not been easy," Adam wrote in his autobiography. "Barden ruled the committee like an old-time plantation-owner—controlling the committee members by refusing to call meetings or scheduling them when he knew that most of the members would be unable to attend because of business in the House. He would then adjourn the meeting for lack of a committee quorum and wait until the members absolutely forced him to schedule another meeting. One year Barden called us for the first committee meeting early in January, naming subcommittees and appointing the members. The next meeting was not called until April and it proved to be brief and unproductive. We met again in July and found that the only item on the agenda was formal adjournment of the committee until the start of the next session in January."

During Barden's ten years only fifty bills introduced to the committee had been passed, and of these only a few had been major bills. But now a Democrat was in the White House and Democrats were the majority party in the House. There was growing emphasis on social legislation and Barden was coming under increasing criticism. If he had been a subcommittee chairman, Adam could have taken advantage of this new, favorable atmosphere for social legislation, but without even a subcommittee chairmanship he was practically powerless.

"He was afraid that he would be blocked out of the Chairmanship until he was seventy or eighty or so," says Skipper Powell. "Barden once threatened to hang on until he died, which could have been at eighty or ninety, at which point my father would have been seventy or eighty. Barden wouldn't even recognize him in committee sessions sometimes, and yet my father hung on. He toyed with the idea of leaving, of taking some other position. 'Maybe I want to be an ambassador,' he'd say. When he was really involved with Puerto Rico in the late 1950s, he toyed with the idea of moving to Puerto Rico and running for the Senate from there. When Kennedy became President he offered my father a Cabinet post. My father was the number three choice, I think; I don't know how firm the offer was, but I was there when he turned it down. He didn't want to leave Congress."

Then it happened: Chairman Graham Barden announced that he would retire at the end of the 1959 session. By all rights, Adam, who had the most seniority on the committee, was next in line for the chairmanship. But there were many who were determined he should not get it. It was not only members of Congress who opposed him. Almost every major newspaper in the country expressed "grave misgivings" about his ability to be an effective chairman, citing as reasons for their doubts his frequent absenteeism, his strong racial attitudes, his long battles over taxes with the Internal Revenue Service.

In the midst of the controversy, yet another problem arose for Adam Powell. In March, 1960, he was interviewed on television and in speaking of police corruption in New York he charged Mrs. Esther James with being a "bagwoman," collecting pay-offs for the police. Mrs. James promptly sued him for libel. When he did not appear at the trial the court found him guilty and ordered him to pay damages of $46,500 to Mrs. James. His lawyers began a series of unsuccessful appeals, during which added penalties brought the judgment to almost $200,000.

"A whole lot of people mentioned the Esther James case as further proof that he was not fit to be chairman," Lewis Upshur points out, "but that case didn't really hurt Adam. White people don't care what happens between a black and another black."

The controversy raged on. "By now the 'get Powell' pattern was very familiar," Adam wrote, "and after several attempted purges I almost knew my opponents' lines by heart. In the early years they were upset because I ate in their private dining room. Now they were upset because I was poaching on what they thought was their own private power structure."

When their attempt to bypass the seniority tradition proved unsuccessful, his opponents tried another tactic, moving that the Education and Labor Committee be divided into two separate committees. In that way, Adam would be chairman of one, but he would not have nearly the power that he would have as chairman of the committee covering both areas. In facing this new tactic, Adam had two powerful allies: John Kennedy who, although he could not intervene directly, let it be known that he supported Adam for the chairmanship, and Sam Rayburn. "If it wasn't for Sam, Adam would either have been chairman of Education or chairman of Labor," says Lewis Upshur. "They didn't want to give him the chairmanship of everything. But Rayburn spoke out, 'No,' he said, 'if anybody in the House is going to have the chairmanship, he's got the seniority.'" In the end, the seniority rule proved too strong, and although the muttering against Adam continued, on March 18, 1961, he was finally sworn in as chairman of the House Education and Labor Committee, the position he had coveted for fifteen years.

Skipper Powell says about his father: "I think of his achievements in two distinctly different areas of time. One was early in the '30s, when he worked here in New York. And then, after he went to Congress—the way Congress is organized you don't really have much power until you're a committee chairman—there was a period in between when he was just as driven and motivated to do things, but when he couldn't really do anything officially in Washington. When he suddenly became chairman, it was like an explosion of activity, and it was just the right time. There was a mood in Congress that made it possible to get a lot more passed than before. He managed to get through eighteen bills during the 87th Congress, which encompassed 1961 and 1962. I still don't see how he did it."

*Representative Powell, Chairman of the
House Education and Labor Committee, holds
a news conference on education legislation.*

"Within five months of my assuming the chairman-ship," Adam wrote, "the minimum-wage bill had passed the House. This was one of the bills that Barden had stifled so long. In just the first session of the 87th Congress twelve education and labor bills became public law, three of them among the eight most important measures passed by the 87th Congress. My committee held twice as many hearings during the 87th Congress as Barden had held in his busiest years, and mine were almost invariably productive, work-ing sessions, whereas Barden had used the hearings to stifle and delay legislation. At the end of 1962 the record showed that my House committee had been more active than any other in the 87th Congress. . . . President Ken-nedy told the press that I had helped, as committee chair-man, to lay the foundation of 'the Great Society.' "

Although as a congressman, Adam was at the peak of his accomplishment during these years, his life in other areas was not running smoothly. His marriage to Yvette was in serious trouble. "She wouldn't leave Puerto Rico to come up here," recalls Pearl Swangson, who had con-tinued to be close to the Powells even after Adam's di-vorce from Hazel Scott. "And he couldn't stay down in Puerto Rico and at the same time carry on his work here —that was the main reason for the break, I know." After a time of visiting Puerto Rico to see Yvette and their baby son once or twice a month, Adam decided theirs wasn't much of a marriage.

Adam was also under attack from Puerto Rican nation-

John F. Kennedy signs the 1961 minimum wage bill into law as Powell (left, rear) looks on.

alists because he supported statehood for the island. Often he longed to escape all these troubles for a while, and when, in 1962, the opportunity arose for him to travel to Europe to study equal opportunities for women in the countries belonging to the Common Market, he decided to go. Two young female secretaries, both unmarried, accompanied him. This was not out of the ordinary for a congressman; many others did, and still do, the same. But Adam Clayton Powell was Adam Clayton Powell, and every trip he took inspired greater interest. And it did seem that he and his secretaries spent more time in European nightclubs than studying equal opportunities for women. The American press called the trip a "shameless junket," and the hue and cry was so alarming that Adam cut short his trip and returned quickly to the United States and to the black community for the support he had always been able to count on.

Adam Powell needed all the help he could get. Enemies in Congress saw their chance to embarrass him, and even those who were not outright enemies were angry at him. The press had begun an investigation of other congressmen's Government-financed trips. Because of Powell, the congressmen grumbled, they might all face public criticism.

"Everybody else did it," Lewis Upshur says. "Senators did it—they took whole planes for their families when they traveled. And one of the congressmen who raised such a fuss about Adam's trip—he had a black butler in

Washington. He took six black people and their wives plus his whole entourage—about nineteen people—along with him on trips and nobody said anything about that."

Leaders in the black community did not approve of Adam's activities during the trip either, but it did not escape their notice that of all the congressmen who took such trips only a black congressman was criticized for doing so. Publicly, they hinted about racism and made statements supporting Adam, as he had known they would. After a while, the furor subsided somewhat. Adam Powell was a powerful man, and his fellow congressmen realized they could not censure him for his "shameless junket" without leaving themselves open to the same criticism. They did not forget what he had done, however, and later they would use it against him.

Hardly a year later Adam became embroiled in another controversy, this time one that directly concerned the black community. By 1963 the mood of the national black community had reached a crossroads. Black people had won certain rights in the courts; they had also managed to desegregate buses and restaurants and other public places in the South through nonviolent demonstrations. But there was still so much to be won, and there was disagreement over what path would lead to success. Martin Luther King, Jr. and other moderate leaders urged black people to continue nonviolent demonstrations to win their rights, to continue working with white people who were willing to help. Others, notably Malcolm X of the Black Muslims, urged greater militancy in demanding equal rights and insisted that no progress could ever be made as long as whites continued to finance and to hold office in civil rights organizations. Adam Powell listened to both sides, as well as to the black community in Harlem and elsewhere in the country, and he decided the people favored greater militancy and the exclusion of whites from civil rights organizations. In the spring of 1963 he came out in support of Malcolm X, angering the moderate black leaders.

It was a bold and risky step for Adam to take. He had no proof that black people favored greater militancy or, more exactly, were ready to engage in a more militant fight for their rights. It just seemed to him that militancy was the only path to take, since nonviolent demonstrations had not earned them enough significant gains. He felt that this young man, Malcolm X, had the potential to be a great black leader in a new, more militant era. He decided to give Malcolm all the help he could.

In those years, Malcolm X was first and foremost a minister of the Nation of Islam, better known as the Black Muslims, a religion and a way of life that preached black pride, self-reliance, and rejection of the white man and his way of thinking.

"When other congregations wouldn't permit Malcolm to hold his church services in their churches, Adam would let him use Abyssinian every Sunday afternoon at 3:00," Lillian Upshur recalls. "The people who attended were mostly from Abyssinian, and he would just talk to them and tell them what he believed in."

"Adam and Malcolm became very close. Malcolm would come around to the church, and we'd see them consulting and talking. Malcolm was like an untouchable at that time. People didn't understand him; they said he was an extremist and they didn't like the way he expressed himself. But Adam understood what he was saying—Adam was ahead of his time in many ways. I remember one time when Malcolm had a rally on the corner of 125th Street. It was November and it was freezing cold. Adam announced in church that we were going to the rally, and when we arrived there was hardly anyone there but Malcolm. Some of his followers were standing around; they had built a speaker's platform and had set up chairs, but the chairs were empty. Adam looked around and said, 'I'll bring the people.' He started walking along the avenue and people started following him. 'Come on, come on,' he said, and more and more people followed him. When he got back to the corner Malcolm embraced him, and Adam got up on the platform and told the people what a fine young man Malcolm was and what he was doing for other young men, helping them when they came out of prison. It was just a great rally."

"Adam loved Malcolm because he was giving kids who didn't care something to care about," says Lewis Upshur. "He told them, 'Don't do criminal things. Study and learn, keep yourselves neat, look upon yourselves with pride, have some pride if you want to be a leader.' "

Lillian Upshur adds, "And when Malcolm was assassinated in 1965 Adam was so upset about it. He said that

Malcolm was emerging as a great leader and he had great confidence in his future. I think that he might have wanted Malcolm to replace him at some time."

Adam was wrong about the mood of the black community in 1963. In the summer of that year a march against segregation in Birmingham, Alabama, was broken up by police dogs and fire hoses. In response to such brutality the country's black people united—not to engage in militant activities but to begin a new, more determined wave of nonviolent demonstrations behind the Reverend Martin Luther King, Jr. Quickly Adam ceased to criticize the moderate civil rights leaders; but casting his lot with Malcolm X had cost him valuable black support—support he would never completely regain.

In December, 1963, Adam was cited for criminal contempt because he had never paid damages to Mrs. Esther James, and the New York Supreme Court issued a warrant for his arrest. Now he could only go to New York when Congress was in session (he had congressional immunity then and could not be arrested) and on Sunday to deliver his sermon at Abyssinian Baptist Church (summonses could not be served in New York on Sundays). He could not even campaign for his own re-election in November, 1964, but he won anyway, by a vote margin of ten-to-one.

Meanwhile, on November 22, 1963, John F. Kennedy was assassinated in Dallas, Texas, and in its shock the country as a whole realized that it was not so much an assassin's bullet as it was the climate of hatred and fear and inequality that had killed a beloved President. In

Congress men began to ask themselves if there wasn't something they could do, some legislation they could pass, to ease this climate. Lyndon B. Johnson, Vice-President under Kennedy who had now assumed the Presidency, felt deeply that civil rights and other social legislation was needed, and he determined to carry out the programs begun by Kennedy.

That is not to say that Adam had an easy time of it as Chairman of the House Education and Labor Committee. He faced great opposition to many of the bills, and yet he usually managed to neutralize that opposition.

"He could put on a façade with white people who could help him, and make some of them his closest friends," says Lillian Upshur, who often observed this talent of Adam's firsthand. "He could use them like they used us. Much of his campaign money always came from rich whites—he had a lot of rich friends—but although they contributed to him they didn't control him. It was politically astute for him to be able to do a favor for them without allowing them to control him or tell him what to do.

"He whipped the Southerners into line," she continues. "They said he was a rare master of getting people to do what he wanted them to do. It was no easy thing for him to influence people, but he knew how to make a deal. He knew what legislation was coming up for a vote, and he knew what they needed and he knew what he needed and was going to get. He was an astute politician, but not for selfish reasons. You'll see from his record that his bills always included the poor and the underprivileged."

In the first five years of his chairmanship Adam successfully guided sixty major laws from his committee to passage. Several of these really benefited black people, and he handled the bills so well that even his critics could not complain. Not one bill from his committee was defeated once it reached the floor of the House of Representatives. These laws included some of the most important social legislation in the history of the United States:

Increasing the minimum wage
The war on poverty
Aid to elementary and secondary education
Barring discrimination in salaries paid to women for the same work performed by men
Assistance for colleges and universities
Manpower development and training for more jobs
Juvenile delinquency and youth offenses control
Vocational rehabilitation
School lunch program
Library services

Adam Powell was everywhere, holding public hearings, attending meetings of his subcommittees, dealing here, trading votes there. He did not confine himself to working only for the bills that came under the jurisdiction of his committee. During those years major civil rights legislation was being considered by Congress, and it was with the help of his tireless efforts that the Civil Rights Act of 1964 and the Voting Rights Act of 1965 were passed. As the number of bills he helped to pass grew, his energy only increased, and even his strongest critics had to admit he was doing a fine job.

"He was always most proud of the poverty legislation," Skipper Powell remembers. "It was not only having written it—he always used to say, 'well, anyone could have written it,'—but having gotten it through, having gotten people to vote for it. He loved the parliamentary maneuverings in Congress. I didn't get down to Washington too often, but when I did he used to love to take me to the House. Relatives of congressmen can stand along the edges, where the cloakroom is, at the far corner. I'd get a hot dog and stand at the door of the cloakroom with him. He would say, 'See him?' pointing to someone sitting there. 'No good. See all those people sitting there? They're all just waiting to vote against the next civil rights bill—it's all they're living for.'

"But he managed to get around people like that. Some political science professors who are designing a new political science course in Boston are using as one of their case studies how some of the early antipoverty bills were passed. In one case a bill was passed by only eight votes, and he got those eight votes in a very clever way. In the original draft of the bill, 1.02 billion dollars was appropriated. He cut the appropriation to 999 million and got those eight votes from people who said they would never vote a billion dollars for poverty. He'd get on the phone to one of the holdouts and say, 'But Sam, we don't have a billion dollars in the bill. Can't you see, we just cut it back!' "

Adam Clayton Powell

On March 18, 1966, President Lyndon Johnson sent a letter to Congressman Powell on the fifth anniversary of his chairmanship.

THE WHITE HOUSE

March 18, 1966

Dear Adam:

The fifth anniversary of your Chairmanship of the House Education and Labor Committee reflects a brilliant record of accomplishment.

It represents the successful reporting to the Congress of 49 pieces of bedrock legislation. And the passage of every one of these bills attests to your ability to get things done.

Even now, these laws which you so effectively guided through the House are finding abundant reward in the lives of our people.

The poverty program is rapidly paving new pathways to progress for those whom the economic vitality of this land had previously bypassed.

The education measures are being translated into fuller opportunities for all our citizens to develop their God-given talents to their fullest potential.

Minimum wage, long a guarantee of a fair return for an honest day's work, has been increased and greatly extended.

And the problems of juvenile delinquency are being met and curtailed by positive and determined action.

Only with progressive leadership could so much have been accomplished by one Committee in so short a time. I speak for the millions of Americans who benefit from these laws when I say that I am truly grateful.

Sincerely yours,
Lyndon B. Johnson

VIII

The year 1966 marked a change in the mood of the black community, a change from the civil rights movement to the Black Power movement. Ever since the late 1950s when two civil rights bills were passed under President Eisenhower, the American South had been alive with civil rights activity, from boycotts by Negroes of segregated buses to sit-ins at segregated lunch counters.

Dr. Martin Luther King and other black leaders in the South had formed the Southern Christian Leadership Conference (SCLC) to organize and direct these protests. In 1960 the SCLC provided funds to a group of Southern black college students to form the Student Nonviolent Coordinating Committee (SNCC). The purpose of the committee would be to organize and direct protests among college students.

From 1960 through 1965 these two groups were the chief forces behind a wave of nonviolent civil rights demonstrations that, although demonstrators were beaten and jailed and even killed, proved remarkably successful. Official discrimination was virtually wiped out in many areas of Southern life, and under President Lyndon B. Johnson two strong civil rights bills, the Civil Rights Act of 1964 and the Voting Rights Act of 1965, were made the law of the land.

By the summer of 1964, SNCC, especially, had decided to concentrate upon registering black voters in the South. The students realized that the blacks in the South could not achieve everything they needed through protest and that having the vote, which would give them political power, could help them achieve other gains. Also, having the vote would insure that they would keep those rights they had won through protest. In the summer of 1964 SNCC launched an intensive voter registration drive in the South—and was rewarded for its efforts with the worst summer of the civil rights years. Countless workers— both black and white—were arrested, scores were beaten, and six were brutally murdered. Despairing, heartsick, the young people of SNCC nevertheless went back to conduct another voter registration drive in the summer of 1965, and were again met with active resistance. Still they remained true to the nonviolent philosophy that had always marked the civil rights movement. But by 1966 many members of SNCC had undergone a radical change in their thinking.

"You can have your nonviolence," they said to the more moderate members of SNCC. "We've tried and look what we've gotten for our efforts. We're not going to turn the other cheek anymore!" A power struggle occurred within SNCC, and when it was over, the faction that favored greater militancy, led by Stokely Carmichael, emerged victorious. SNCC would have a new image, Carmichael declared, and a new rallying cry was needed. Until then the rallying cry had been, "We Shall Overcome!" In the summer of 1966 Stokely Carmichael issued a new call: "Black Power!"

For Carmichael and those who supported him, Black Power was an excellent slogan because it could mean many things to many people, ranging from an equal share to armed revolution. It would bring the black community together by offering something to everyone. But the new SNCC, when interviewed by reporters, seemed to have no specific goals outlined for the future and no specific definition for Black Power. When Adam recognized this uncertainty he quickly took steps to harness the forces of this new militant movement.

He saw great possibilities in the Black Power idea, but he also recognized that the slogan and the movement needed to be defined, for blacks as well as whites. Already Black Power was bringing frightening images to the minds of whites and moderate blacks—images of angry blacks seizing power through violence. Adam felt that the positive, constructive possibilities of Black Power should be discussed. Shortly after the slogan rang across the country, Adam called a conference of national black leaders to discuss black power.

"You know, Black Power was really his thing," Gwen Jones, who arranged that conference, says. "The first Black Power conference was held in the Hearing Room of the House. We excluded all white press, and they were very upset with us. But you see, the whole reason for the conference was to arrive at some kind of unity of purpose, some agreed-upon definition of the slogan, some mutually agreeable future goals. But if we had let the white press in, that would never have happened. There were all kinds of blacks there, from moderates to militants, and anything we said could have been interpreted by the white press as evidence of differences among us. We didn't need that kind of divisive propaganda. Of course we were all different, but then whites don't realize that blacks aren't all alike—we range from the militant to the extreme right— and they would have interpreted natural differences of opinion as serious conflicts."

Little came of that conference, however, and from then on Adam Powell had little officially to do with the Black Power movement. Some speculated that the conference itself was not important to Adam and that he had simply wished to give the militants a chance to cool off. Others felt that he had been excluded from leadership of the movement by people like Carmichael, who were young and critical of any leader who had worked within the system.

They were saying to older black leaders, "Your time is gone; now our time has come."

According to Gwen Jones, Adam's brief involvement with the Black Power movement gave his enemies in Congress yet more ammunition against him. "The first Black Power conference," she says, "was the beginning of the trouble."

The trouble was a serious move by certain members of Congress to bar Adam from the House, and it began in 1966. In September the House set up a special subcommittee, headed by Wayne Hays of Ohio, to investigate the records of the Education and Labor Committee and the activities of its chairman. The reasons given were Adam's absenteeism, the warrant for his arrest that was still out in New York, and charges that he spent his committee's monies improperly, putting his relatives on the congressional payroll and charging their pleasure trips and his own on the congressional expense account. Adam pleaded poor health as the reason for many of his absences, but to the other accusations he responded with charges of racism. "I do not do any more than any other member of Congress, and by the Grace of God, I'll not do less!" he cried.

He did not try to save himself by denying the charges or by making any deals. He challenged his accusers to prove he was any more guilty than they.

"I think if he could have been sold or bought, he wouldn't have had a problem," Gwen Jones says. "But he was independent—he would say what he thought in no uncertain terms—and he was black. He was getting too close to real power. His next move would have been to Speaker of the House, and they would not have a black man, no matter how fair, as Speaker of the House."

Adam later wrote: "The hypocrisy of the entire Hays Committee action passed almost unnoticed by the world at large, but within Congress the members were aware of it. I refused to be meek and let them off the hook easily. If I had to go down, I was going down swinging. When I was asked to appear before the Hays Committee, I stipulated that I would do so only if I were allowed the right to cross-examine witnesses, including congressmen. This sounds like a basic right, inherent in the American judicial system. But my fellow lawmakers knew very well that if I started to ask them questions, we could easily end up drawing lots to see who was the guilty congressman who should be punished. I could have asked Hays himself who paid for the almost fifty flights between Washington and his home in Ohio. Needless to say, my request was denied."

After this, Adam made little attempt to defend himself during the committee investigation. He remained out of the country while those who wished to strip him of his chairmanship and House seat worked eagerly on. They were aided by Yvette Flores Diago Powell, who traveled to Washington, expenses paid by Congress, to testify against her husband. "I never thought the day would come when Yvette would turn on me," Adam wrote in his autobiography. Not until January, 1967, did he return to Congress, where one of the first items on the agenda was the Powell case.

First, they stripped him of the chairmanship of the House Education and Labor Committee. By vote of 140 to 70 a closed Democratic caucus removed him as chairman and named the ranking member of the committee, Carl Perkins, as the new chairman. The next day the entire House voted 364 to 64 to exclude Adam from his seat in Congress until a new committee investigated his fitness as a congressman.

"At this point I formed my own committee," Adam wrote in his autobiography, "the best civil rights lawyers I could find. . . . This group represented the finest collection of legal minds that could be assembled. And they worked without a fee, simply for justice. While the members of the congressional committee were deciding if, in their opinion, I was 'fit to serve,' I was determined to prove that the Constitution of the United States sets only three qualifications for House service—age, citizenship, and residence. According to the Constitution a man (or woman) is fit to serve in Congress as long as he is twenty-five years of age, a citizen of the United States, and a resident of the state in question. That was the legal issue. Equally important was the moral issue: I had been elected by an overwhelming majority of the people in my district —at the very height of the virulent anti-Powell campaign that was carried on in every newspaper and magazine in the country."

The black community was definitely behind Adam.

*Adam Powell leaves the Capitol amid a crowd
of supporters after being denied his seat by the
House of Representatives in January, 1967.*

From the man-on-the-street to moderate and militant leaders, every black who voiced an opinion said the same thing: If Adam Powell were not black, none of this would be happening. If his conduct as a congressman is being investigated, then so should that of every other congressman. But though he had the support of the black community and the support of the best legal minds in the country, Adam realized that he could not win, at least not this round of the fight. Because of his controversial stands, he had accumulated many enemies in Congress through the years. The Republicans had always been against him, and he was quite certain that the Democrats were now against him as well. As he reflected, "I had realized that there had been some realignment of power when, in September of 1966, I had attended the signing of the War on Poverty bill in President Johnson's office. The President refused to shake my hand when I arrived, and his entire attitude toward me was one of complete detachment—as if I were already a dead man and he would have preferred not to have a corpse in his office."

It did not take long for the new special committee to decide that Adam Powell was unfit to be a Congressman. But although Adam could not have held much hope of a favorable vote, many had expected that he would at least make a strong speech on his own behalf. But when he rose to speak, he rambled on, mumbling something about skeletons in everyone's closet and how he, at least, would be able to sleep that night. Where was the famous oratorial power for which this preacher–politician was known?

Adam Powell seemed a beaten man.

"That was a very sad day," Hattie Dodson remembers. "I told my husband, 'You go. I don't think I could stand it.' So my husband went, and later he told me, 'Hattie, when I opened that door after they had refused him his seat, Adam turned around and we just embraced.' He was so glad to see a close friend who'd come down to be with him. I think it meant a lot."

Over a thousand people from Harlem had journeyed to Washington to show their support of their congressman, and when they heard of the vote they threatened to "burn the town down." Militant and moderate black leaders alike denounced the House action. Adam's lawyers, sure the exclusion was unconditional, began preparing to take the case to court.

Adam himself was tired and discouraged, and he needed time to think.

Skipper Powell recalls, "He was disappointed in individual congressmen rather than in the Congress as a whole. We would talk about the exclusion and I would be livid, asking, 'How could you let Congress do that?' But he was not upset at Congress as a body. He would say, 'Well, I can't understand how so-and-so could be here at the house just three weeks before the vote and vow to support me and then vote against me.' "

What Adam needed most at this point was peace, and the only place in the world, it seemed, where he could find peace was a small island in the Bahamas, about six miles off Miami, Florida. Bimini.

IX

"Adam first went to Bimini in about 1963," remembers Lewis Upshur. "He was fishing off some other island in the Bahamas, uninhabited, with some other men, and one of them told him about Bimini. He'd read about it and heard about how good the fishing was around Bimini, so he went there to see for himself. He fished there regularly for about a year and a half, and then he decided to build a house there. Wherever he went, Adam built a house."

"There's nothing much on Bimini," adds Lillian Upshur. "It's just one long strip of land called North Bimini, and then another strip of land called South Bimini—that's where his house was. But the fishing was great, and he was a great fisherman. He even claimed that Skipper had a birthmark shaped like a fish. He loved the sea, and he would take us in his boat all the way out from Bimini to where the Gulf starts and show us how the water was blue here and red over there. He would take us out fishing and we'd catch all kinds of beautiful fish, and he would tell us what each one was and whether or not we should throw it back. He would show us how to hold the reel and what bait to use—we always used conch meat.

"His boat was called *Adam's Fancy*, and it was a small boat. We ran into a storm once, it came up suddenly, and there was something jutting out into the water, a rock or something, and Adam took the wheel away from his captain and guided the boat right around it. And one time we were on the boat and something burst in the motor and of course flooded it. We were in very deep water, and while he was bailing out he said, 'Mighty deep, this water, and you know, if we sank you wouldn't live a minute, because there are barracudas down there.' "

Before Adam started going to Bimini, it was strictly a fishing resort for whites. The native Biminians were not allowed into the big fishing clubs except as servants. Adam "integrated" fishing on Bimini, frequenting the big fishing clubs, participating in—and winning—the numerous tournaments. He had little trouble in gaining entrance—how could you keep out a U.S. congressman? Also, he brought the clubs more business than they had ever enjoyed before. Bimini was also not very well known, which was not a good situation for an island whose only economy is its tourist trade. But Adam changed all that.

Adam Clayton Powell, Jr. on his fishing boat, Adam's Fancy

"In my opinion the publicity he gave the islanders was worth more than all the travel agents in the world," says Holman McDonald, a Bimini resident for some forty years who knew Adam from 1965 on. "During his stay here we had men like Martin Luther King, Jr., Stokely Carmichael, Rap Brown, and Senator Mike Mansfield come to visit him. He was always bringing people down here, and he held press conferences. I know times when there were as many as a hundred to a hundred and fifty reporters here, writers from all over the world. When an island as small as Bimini is covered by radio and television all over the United States—CBS, ABC, and NBC all in one day—that gives you a lot of publicity."

The publicity he brought to Bimini was an indirect gift from Adam to its people, but he gave many direct gifts as well. "They didn't have any good water," says Lewis Upshur, "and he set it up so they could have machinery to purify the water coming out of the ocean. He got electricity put in."

Adam was also concerned that the people's diet was not very good. "Somehow or other, he didn't know why, they could not raise chickens," says Lillian Upshur, "and there were certain vegetables they could not raise. He started a garden right there on the beach, and of course the heat and sun just dried it up. We said, 'Now you see why they can't grow vegetables.' So he made arrangements so they could go to Miami and get their food and bring it back for a special rate. Any other time it costs $18.00 to fly over to the mainland, but now they have a special

Adam Powell and Stokely Carmichael on a Bimini street

card so they can go over and bring back their vegetables.

"There was no hospital, no clinic, not even a doctor down there," Lillian Upshur continues, "so what did Adam do? He made arrangements with Miami Memorial General Hospital whereby mothers can get prenatal care and can have their children in a hospital. And once a month he'd have a doctor and a nurse come to the island, and any children who needed care would receive medication."

Lewis Upshur adds, "A lot of the children didn't have sneakers, any kind of shoes, so Adam sent away to Sears and Roebuck and got cases and cases of shoes for kids, and shorts, too. He bought the boys baseballs and uniforms and they had a baseball team and played the teams from all the islands in the Bahamas. They won the championship when he was there."

Eric Vincent Dawkins, Adam's boat captain, remembers a severe storm on the island. "Everything was flooded and he sent for food and supplies from Miami. Some of the water was contaminated, so he asked the U.S. Coast Guard to fly water in fresh until things were straightened out. I remember very clearly—it was 1965, the first full year he stayed in the house down here. He didn't stay in his house the first night of the storm; he stayed in the church with the mothers and the babies. He stayed up with them all night—didn't even go to see about his own house."

Adam also addressed himself to education on the island. Holman McDonald, whose wife is a schoolteacher on Bimini, and who is a member of the Bimini school board, recalls, "One time when an epidemic was threatening the Bahamas and we had to close the school, Powell went all out. After we had gotten the Government to renovate the school with running water and other modern facilities, we had a meeting in the schoolhouse. He promised he would do what he could to give the children better equipment, and he went off to Washington. The first shipment of school supplies that Mr. Powell sent to Bimini was valued at $30,000. We even had projectors and other audiovisual machines—he more or less furnished the school. We had so many supplies that we had to send some to Nassau. And when he sent all this equipment, he didn't send it alone. He sent over two teachers from California, people who specialize in this sort of equipment, to set up the machines and show the teachers how to operate them.

"He was Chairman of the Education and Labor Committee in the United States, and he had connections. He could go to these manufacturers and say I want so-and-so —it was more or less donations. But he didn't have to do it. Bimini education wasn't really his problem, because Bimini is a British island."

During the time when he had traveled to Puerto Rico once or twice a month to see Yvette and their son, Adam had met Corinne Huff who, as Miss Ohio, had been the first black contestant from America in the Miss Universe contest. By the time he had begun to stay in Bimini, Adam and Huffi, as he called her, were inseparable, and the house in South Bimini was in Huffi's name. It was a small cinder-block house of three or four rooms, set upon a hill overlooking the sea. Adam taught Huffi to fish, and every morning they would go out fishing for three, sometimes four hours.

"Normally they would go out around 10:30 or 11:00," recalls Eric Vincent Dawkins, who started out as a mechanic for Adam's boat and eventually became its captain, "unless there was a tournament, then you have to leave at 9:00. He won just about every tournament. I told him on many occasions, 'Why don't you just anchor the boat and stay all night? Since I want to go in and you still want to fish, why don't you anchor the boat and I'll go to sleep, and you can fish?' That's the only way I could get him to go in sometimes. He used to call himself the Old Man of the Sea."

Although numerous kinds of fish can be found in the waters surrounding Bimini, Adam especially liked fishing for wahoo. Emmanuel Rolle, who operates a charter fishing boat and a sort of general store on Bimini, has many stories to tell about Adam's quest for wahoo: "Mr. Powell and I had a bet in 1968 about catching wahoo—who would catch the most in one season. He caught 140 wahoo that season, brought them in, gave them away to people, sent them to friends on the mainland. I only caught 114. But the difference between Mr. Powell and me was that he was his own boss, he could go fishing every day. I could only fish when I had customers. He was a good sportsman because he admitted that, with the number of days I fished compared to the number of days he fished, I beat him by 25 per cent. He paid the bet of $100 without any argument.

"When he wasn't fishing, or when he'd come in from fishing, he'd play dominoes at the End-of-the-World Bar. The boys there liked to play dominoes, and he liked to mix with the boys, sit down and chat."

The End-of-the-World Bar is a little ramshackle place, its right end settled lower than its left. Paint peels from its weather-beaten clapboards, and its always open doorway is black against the sandy, sun-beaten road. Did whoever named it forsee that it would someday look like the end of the world?

"He said it reminded him of something about home," says Eric Dawkins. "Maybe some place he used to go before. Once he said, 'That's where you meet all the soul brothers.' You could put it that he meant the people at the End-of-the-World were like people back in Harlem. He liked to go places that people say don't count."

Adam never fished on Sundays, nor did he play dominoes. On Sundays when he was on Bimini he preached. Days before signs would be nailed on the coconut trees: "Reverend Powell is going to preach Sunday," and Sunday afternoon he would mount the steps of the Bimini Hotel and deliver a sermon as moving and powerful as any he had delivered from the pulpit of Abyssinian Baptist Church.

"He used to hold services at the Bimini Hotel every Sunday afternoon," says Holman McDonald, "and after

Sunday School the children traveled down here to the service. And on Father's Day, or any day for men in the church, he was always invited to talk to the men. He would give them a lecture, and it was always an inspiration for the upstanding men of the island, because he would give you food for thought, and he'd close it each time with a big joke—and everybody would laugh."

Easter Sunday was a special day, which everyone on the island celebrated. "He would always want us to be there during Easter week," says Lillian Upshur. "On Easter Sunday he would hold a special service, and then there would be a big picnic and everybody on the island would cook a favorite dish. Adam would go around and eat a little bit of everybody's, saying, 'Oh, it's so good!' He would taste everything, and be so warm, and everybody just loved him."

She adds, "When he knew we were coming down, we would have to stop in Miami first and go to a wholesale place to get meat, collard greens, and chitlins. They would put it all in cases and take it to the plane bound for Bimini. Adam had a deep freezer, and he had everything in it labeled: 'collard greens,' 'chitlins' . . ."

Adam Powell in self-imposed exile, having to import his "soul food," setting himself up as a benevolent king to the people of Bimini—that's how some would see him. But that's not the way it really was. Certainly, he had to obtain collard greens and chitlins from the mainland, but that did not mean Bimini was not a real home. The people of Bimini needed help in many ways, but Adam did not see them in a paternal way, as people to be "uplifted," but as friends.

"He was a guy you could go to and talk to anytime," says Eric Dawkins. "He never pushed you to the side or be too busy. And he'd never hesitate to introduce anyone here to any of the dignitaries from the North. He'd always take them around to different places and introduce them, saying, 'This is so-and-so; these are my friends.' "

As Adam spent more and more time in Bimini, he became very interested in Bahamian politics. The Bahamas were a British commonwealth, and while most of their population was black, they were governed and economically controlled by the small white population. "He would say how fortunate the Bahamian people were," say Holman McDonald. "With 85 per cent of the population of the Bahamas being black and only 15 per cent white, it was always his opinion that we had a better chance to govern our country than black people had in the United States. When he first came down here the United Bahamian party was in power, and they didn't like Adam Powell's philosophly and his urging independence for the Bahamas. One time they threatened to deport him, but he was a resident, so they really couldn't do anything. Then when the Progressive Labor party gained power, and Prime Minister Pindling came in, Mr. Powell became very closely associated with Pindling."

Before Pindling had become Prime Minister, he had been Adam's lawyer, so actually the two had been closely associated before. But having the Prime Minister of the Bahamas as his friend was definitely an advantage for Adam. It was an ace-in-the-hole, if he ever wanted to use it.

"He had this thought of either running for office there in the Bahamas, or—something that really amused him— of becoming Bahamian Ambassador to the United States," Skipper Powell says. The people of Bimini would have loved that, for they loved Adam Powell. He, in turn, loved them.

Adam was happy in Bimini, happier than he had been in a long time. Eric Dawkins recalls, "Every time he went away for two or three months, he would come back looking pale. But after a couple weeks down here he'd look like Adam again. I don't know whether it was the pressure in the North or what, but when he was down here he was more relaxed."

Even on Bimini, though, Adam experienced unhappiness. Huffi and Patrick Brown, a native of Bimini, fell in love, and thus he lost yet another woman. "That was a big shock," recalls Eric Dawkins. "He really loved her, and he felt she had double-crossed him. He was very disappointed and depressed, and some of us who were very close to him had a talk with him, tried to get his morale back."

Shortly thereafter, Adam met Darlene Exposé in Washington. A native of Hattiesburg, Mississippi, who had picked cotton when she was younger, Darlene Exposé had been working for congressmen on Capitol Hill in Washington for four years when she met Adam. Soon Adam and Darlene had fallen in love. The house on South Bimini had been in Corinne Huff's name and belonged to her, so Adam had another house built. This one, also a small cinder-block structure, was built on the north end of South Bimini, just across the small inlet that separates North and South Bimini. The rowboat which they used to cross the inlet was named *Darlene*. A pretty, quiet girl, Darlene would prove a great comfort to Adam in many ways.

They sought him out in Bimini, the newsmen. Sometimes he wanted them there, when he wished to hold news conferences, for example, but sometimes he wanted to be alone, and they wouldn't allow him to be.

"When the court barred him from New York [because of the Esther James case], the press were all over the place," says Eric Dawkins. "Here it is your own backyard—all these people, cameras, television—you didn't know who was who."

One photograph carried in practically every newspaper across the United States showed Adam walking toward his house with a shotgun in his hand. The caption reads as if he were defending himself from the United States law. "I was in on that," says Dawkins. "Adam was out on the boat. Two reporters from ABC in New York rented a boat to chase him and take pictures. Some of us saw this, and we went out in a small boat to let him know what was going on. After warning him we took the small boat back in and drove out to the eastern end of South Bimini. We picked him up and drove him to the house. When we reached the house, the reporters were there with their cameras. Adam kept a rifle on the boat and when we picked him up we took the rifle, too. When we got to the house I was supposed to carry the rifle inside, but in all the excitement Adam picked up the rifle himself and went into the house."

Adam did not seem to want to return to the United States after his exclusion from Congress. "They want me to go back, but I'm not going," he told Lillian and Lewis Upshur. "What do you want to go back there for? You stay here in Bimini with me."

Lewis Upshur did not want to live in Bimini, but he understood why Adam didn't want to go back to the United States. "I said, 'Adam, why don't you give it all up? You did enough for the people; they don't appreciate it, your church doesn't appreciate it.' If it hadn't been for Lillian, Adam would never have run for Congress in the special election in April, 1967. She put his name in. He wouldn't tell her to do it or not. She kept asking him and he wouldn't say anything. And, bless the Lord, when we got back to New York, who put the man's name in? It was she, because he definitely wasn't going to run."

The special election was held after Adam's ouster from Congress because the people of the 18th Congressional District were without representation. "When the results of the voting were announced that April," Adam later wrote, "I felt as humble as any man under God could feel. I was a Congressman who had been excluded from the 90th Congress; there was no possible way I could serve, and yet the people of Harlem had elected me again—by a margin of seven to one. As a public protest, to put forever on record their feelings regarding the exclusion, an entire Congressional district had decided to go without representation in Washington for two years."

"I was sure he would come back once we had won that election," says Lillian Upshur.

But she was wrong. He never presented his certificate of victory to Congress.

"He felt that he had been let down," says C. D. King. "He told me that he didn't understand why there wasn't an uprising in Harlem about the way Congress had treated him. I think he had about decided that the people had forsaken him."

For several more months Adam stayed on Bimini and did not return to the United States.

Early in 1968 Adam Powell suddenly began to climb out of the well of despair into which he had fallen since his ouster from Congress. After years of appeals, a compromise was effected in the Esther James case. It was agreed that if Adam would pay the original penalty all additional penalties would be dropped. He began to pay the damages the court had awarded Mrs. Esther James, and thus the court voided its warrant for his arrest. For the first time in over four years he was free to return to Harlem.

He did not return immediately. First he went on a speaking tour, visiting the major colleges in the country. He needed reassurance that he was still respected, that he was still considered an important black leader, before he could face the people of Harlem. He received that reassurance on his college tour. "I hold one record not many speakers can match," he wrote in his autobiography. "I have never been shouted down or had a session of mine disrupted on any campus. I know of several governors who would like to be able to say the same thing." Confidence restored by the lecture tour, Adam returned to New York, arriving quietly late at night. He would get a good night's sleep; then he would go to the people.

"Look who's here! Look who's back in town!" Adam cried as he walked along Seventh Avenue north from 125th Street the next morning. It was as if he'd never been away. Laughing, shouting his favorite slogan, *Keep the Faith*, he became the leader of a spontaneous, happy parade by the time he had completed the first block. He was still the Pied Piper of Harlem, even though he had stayed away from home much too long.

"Today marks the opening of my campaign for re-election," he told the crowd.

"You got some tough competition," someone called out.

"Hah!" cried Adam. "Any nigger crazy enough to run against me is the first nigger to be crucified in the North!"

Same old Adam. The crowd loved it.

But despite the warm welcome, Adam's long absence from the community had caused him to lose political support, and he had to campaign vigorously for the Democratic primary in June. Winning the primary, he campaigned hard for the November election, which he won handily, although his vote margin was smaller than it had ever been

*In January, 1968, nearly a year after being
denied his House seat, Powell prepares to march
through Los Angeles' Watts district.*

in the past. The important thing, though, was that he had won. "He said to me that he was going to win that 1968 election," Emmanuel Rolle recalls, "that he was going to get back into Congress."

In January, 1969, Adam Powell stood on the floor of the House of Representatives and took the oath of office. It was the twelfth time he had taken that oath, and yet in many ways it seemed like the first. He had been absent for two years—during which time the seat of the representative from Harlem had been vacant—and he was starting with no more power, officially, than any freshman congressman. The House had stripped him of his twenty-two years seniority. In addition, his fellow congressmen had agreed to admit him only after he had consented to pay a $25,000 fine for "gross misconduct."

Naturally Adam's seating was the subject of much controversy in Washington and received considerable news coverage, but once the 91st Congress got down to business his presence attracted little unusual attention. That was fine with Adam. He did not wish to become involved in any controversy, and he was tired from the months of campaigning. When he was working, he divided his time between Washington and New York, and as often as possible he returned to Bimini. He happened to be in Bimini when the United States Supreme Court announced its decision in the Powell exclusion case.

Ever since Congress had denied him his seat in 1967, Adam's lawyers had been appealing the case in every court that would hear them until finally they had carried it to the highest court in the land. On July 16, 1969, the Supreme Court ruled that Congress had acted unconstitutionally in denying Adam Powell his seat because the congressional session had not yet begun. If he had been barred in the middle of a session it would have been a different matter. But because he had just been reelected to his seat in November, 1966, Congress had no right to prevent him from taking it when the new congressional session began in January, 1967. The Court left unresolved the question of whether or not Congress owed him the salary for the two years during which he had been wrongfully excluded and the question of whether or not Congress had been within its rights to strip him of his seniority and to fine him $25,000. The main thing, though, was that the Supreme Court had found Congress had acted unconstitutionally in excluding Adam Powell, and the news created a furor.

Numerous congressmen publicly protested the Court's decision, and reporters fell over each other to reach Bimini to get a statement from the subject of the case. They found a smiling but subdued Powell, who did not seem very elated by his victory. In earlier years he would have puffed on a big cigar and shaken hands and slapped people on the back and posed for photographers and made witty remarks into the sea of microphones. Now, all he said was, "Adam Powell doesn't matter . . . it's a victory for the American people." The reporters looked questioningly at one another. Where was the old Adam Powell? Had all the fight gone out of him?

149]

*Adam Clayton Powell, Jr., expresses satisfaction
at the 1969 Supreme Court decision that he was
illegally removed from his House seat.*

Adam was sixty years old and he had been fighting for a long time, and although few people realized it, he was very sick. Later that summer he was told that more cancer had been found and there followed many months of treatment in New York before the spread of the disease appeared to be halted. After being discharged from the hospital, Adam returned again to Bimini, where his friends urged him to stay. But another congressional election was coming up, in November of 1970, and Adam intended to run once more.

"I had hoped that he would just resign," says Hattie Dodson, "but how can a man of his brilliance with his pride, give up, even though he knows himself that he wants to?"

In the Democratic primary in June, Adam faced the stiffest competition he had ever come up against. State Assemblyman Charles B. Rangel, an articulate spokesman for black people who had acquired a reputation as an activist in the state legislature, wanted Adam's seat. He waged a vigorous, hard-hitting campaign, stressing Adam's long absences from the community, his failure to help the people of Harlem in any meaningful way in the last few years, and his seeming lack of concern about campaigning for the primary. "He was sick and he didn't feel like campaigning," says Hattie Dodson. "He was possibly sicker than the people knew. I think if he had been able to campaign a little . . ."

Lillian Upshur recalls vividly that primary election and what came after. "We were at the Alfred Isaacs Democratic Club and it had come over the radio that Adam had won, so he set off for Rangel's headquarters to tell the man he'd fought a good fight. But first he stopped off at another one of his headquarters, and there he found out that he had lost. The margin was only 150 votes, and we couldn't believe it. We started checking all of the voting machines, and we found so many discrepancies in the voting. We had them all documented, and we filed briefs, and we were supposed to go to court. Rangel had to be served with a subpoena, and it was issued, but it was never delivered to him. He just decided to go to Atlantic City and never received it although it was tacked to his door. Our suit was denied and we never did get our day in court. That just broke Adam up, because we had the proof and we could have gotten another primary election."

Now the only way Adam could get on the ballot in November was to run as an Independent, and to be eligible he had to collect signatures of 3,000 voters in the district. As the three other losing candidates had announced their support of Adam as an Independent, the task did not seem impossible. Immediately his staff went to work collecting signatures, and when the deadline arrived, Adam presented 3,377 names. Rangel challenged the validity of the signatures, and the investigation that followed revealed that 2,001 of names were not listed on the district voting lists. That made Adam's petition 1,624 short of the 3,000 required names, and Adam ineligible to run as an Independent. There is still disagreement over those signatures and the manner in which Adam was ruled ineligible, but to Adam's supporters the real issue was the validity of 1,400 of Charles Rangel's votes in the June primary.

"If it had really gone to court, Adam would have won," insists Lillian Upshur. "That's why he never conceded."

Lewis Upshur adds, "Adam died never conceding that he'd lost."

On November 3, 1970, Charles Rangel outpolled his opponents to win election to the House of Representatives and to the seat that Adam had held, except for the two years when he had been denied it, for twenty-four years. It was, as Charles Rangel put it, "the end of an era."

Gwen Jones feels that the era of Adam Clayton Powell really ended when he was expelled from Congress. "He was a different person, a very bitter man. You couldn't tell it from his way of speaking—only sometimes could you see how discouraged and bitter he really was. He had given so much, and he didn't have to, he could have turned his back on the people and not bothered at all."

After being ruled ineligible for the 1970 election, he felt no need to bother at all. He stayed on Bimini and rarely returned to Harlem or even to the United States.

"He tried several times to resign as pastor of Abyssinian," says Gwen Jones, "and they refused to take his resignation. I think the last time it was obvious that they would have to accept it, but they accepted it with the understanding that he would become pastor emeritus and be available for consultation and come in as often as he felt he wanted to."

"Adam wanted me to retire when he retired," says Reverend David Licorish, "but after I explained to him that I needed the salary the Church paid me, he admitted that was true and dropped the subject. Miss Dodson wanted him to name a successor, but he said, 'No, I'm not naming any successor.' Adam had not thought of leaving, even though he had retired. He did not know, or want to admit, how sick he was."

Skipper Powell visited his father several times after he returned to Bimini for good, and it pained him to see how ill his father was. But what was more painful was that Adam Powell had to watch, powerless, while so much of his work was undone.

"The last time I was in Bimini we were watching a TV newscast and they announced that the House Health, Education and Welfare appropriation had been cut, and he was saying, 'Oh, that means they're going to really kill the obligated funds.' I remember asking, 'What's there, then, to show for all that happened in the early '60s? Here it is 1972, and it's like we're back in the '30s again. They're hiring transit workers by means of a system of lists again, and they hire from the lists in such a way that very few black people are hired.' He would take the congressional directory and point out the programs where they weren't spending the money, where the lowest percentage of the authorized money was being spent. Inevitably they'd be the programs for blacks, Indians, Mexican Americans— all the programs for poor people were the ones that weren't being funded. I asked again, 'What's left after all this?' and he said, 'Well, I don't know if there's anything left except the framework, the laws. If people don't spend the monies for the programs and don't use the laws the way they were meant to be used, there isn't much left.' He ended by being rather discouraged. At one point he said, 'Oh, I just don't know where people are now. Everyone seems to be just sort of sitting back; either they've got a little and they're holding onto it, or they've got nothing, and they don't know what to do.'

"Those last few times," Skipper Powell continues, "my father talked a lot about the '30s and the '60s—those two distinct periods in his life when he got so much accomplished. The things he did during those years were the things he talked about most. He was afraid that people would not remember. . . ."

In March, 1972, Adam, suffering from complications from an earlier prostate operation, was rushed by helicopter from Bimini to a Miami hospital. "Everybody here was concerned," recalls Emmanuel Rolle. "Bulletins were coming over on his condition and I don't think there was one person on the island who didn't listen." Across the United States, Americans listened to the hospital bulletins.

Adam Powell died on April 4, 1972, and around the world black people mourned. His funeral was held in the church that had been his for nearly four decades. Blacks from across the country came to file quietly past his bier, but most of the 100,000 people who came to pay their last respects had to travel only a few blocks; after a six-year, self-imposed exile, Adam Clayton Powell had returned to Harlem.

Many of the mourners remembered when his had been almost the sole voice for black Americans. They were, as the New York *Amsterdam News* noted, "mostly the old-timers and the middle-aged," those to whom Adam had been "the man, the spirit, the political force, and preacher *extraordinaire* who in the 1930s, '40s, and '50s was Harlem's Black Knight in shining armor." The young came as well but many looked on curiously, unable to understand what this man had represented to their people.

Harlem had changed, and although many spoke of the funeral as "Adam come home," it was over the clear blue waters of Bimini that his ashes were scattered, as he had wished.

Afterword

Adam Clayton Powell, Jr.—for a quarter of a century he served in one of the highest offices in the land and, as Chairman of the House Education and Labor Committee, enjoyed more power than any other black man before or since has attained. For some forty years he worked to better the lives of black people, from organizing free soup kitchens to pushing civil rights legislation through Congress. For all this, many feel that he never realized his full potential for public service. They say this was due to his own weaknesses. They are forgetting, however, the climate of America during much of his public career.

Says Reverend David Licorish, "We must measure the success of the man by the tide that he's had to stem, and the high walls of prejudice he's had to scale. The fight is on, and it is tragic that Adam died so prematurely with so many things on his mind. To me, it is tragic that a man who blew such a loud trumpet was forced to close out his life with such a small flute."

Gwen Jones also remembers the barriers that Adam had to break down. "Those of us who grew up in the Depression and knew what it was like then for black people appreciate more what he did than those who did not," she says. "We had a street meeting the Monday after his death, and we found that so many people did not understand what he had done. Many had no notion that this man was an historic figure; they had no notion of his minimum wage laws, no notion of what he had done for Senior Citizens, no notion of any of his education bills—60 laws, and they had no notion of any of them."

Throughout Adam Powell's career, and particularly in the later years, his accomplishments tended to be overshadowed in the press by his flamboyance and his excesses. For this reason many people—especially those who did not live through the '30s and '40s—were unaware of how important were his contributions to black people. It was he, probably more than any other individual, who laid the groundwork for the progress black Americans have made toward equal rights and power in America from demonstrating for jobs in Harlem during the Depression to the civil rights legislation of the Sixties.

"I'm so sorry he died young before he could enjoy the fruits of his labor," says Pearl Swangson. "I think he

should be here now, to see things grow, to see the doors that had been boarded up opened. 'They cannot do without us,' he said. 'And maybe we can't do without them.' "

Many whites agreed with Adam on that, although they had reservations about his flamboyance and the way he went about getting things done. But Adam's flamboyance, his "I answer only to myself" attitude, was more than just his natural style. When necessary, he knew how to use this façade in a brilliantly calculated manner. Without it he could never have accomplished what he did, and many people, white and black, who are in positions of power recognize that.

Skipper Powell often goes to Washington, the city he came to know so well when he was "the Chairman's son." "Once, not long ago," he says, "I stopped in to see one committee chairman who knew my father rather well. He sort of shook his head and said, 'A lot of people thought your father was really outrageous. What we need around here are more people who are outrageous.' "

Appendix A

Without the help of the eleven people who are briefly identified here, this book could not have been written. Their memories and perceptions were invaluable, and it is through them and others like them that Adam Powell, the man, will live on.

Eric Vincent Dawkins

Eric Vincent Dawkins was Adam Powell's boat captain on Bimini during his last three years, but he knew Adam from 1963 on, when the congressman first began to visit Bimini. In some ways Dawkins was closer to Powell during his last years than anyone else, for in those years the real Adam Powell was the man who lived on Bimini.

161]

Hattie Dodson

Hattie Dodson knew Adam Powell for forty years. When they were children they played together, and when they grew up they worked together. As one of his secretaries, she traveled with him to Washington when he was elected to Congress, later returning to work in Powell's New York office. Hattie Dodson used to transcribe and catalogue all of Adam Powell's sermons and send them to Washington.

C. D. King

C. D. King was Adam Powell's brother-in-law. He married Blanche Powell when she was sixteen and Adam was only six. Although he was not closely involved with Adam, King's ties with the Powell family gave him a view of Adam, particularly in his boyhood years, which some of his close business associates did not have the opportunity to share.

The Reverend David Licorish

The Reverend David Licorish was associate pastor of Abyssinian Baptist Church for twenty-eight years. As such, he worked very closely with Adam Clayton Powell, Jr.; but the relationship between the two men went beyond a business association. They trusted each other; in fact, as long as Adam was pastor of the Abyssinian Baptist Church, Licorish was assured of his own position. Early in the summer of 1972, he was retired from Abyssinian.

Gwen Jones

Gwen Jones has spent most of her life working in the Abyssinian Baptist Church. When Adam Clayton Powell,

Sr. was pastor, she worked for him and when Adam, Jr. came home from college, he became her boss. Though she was never formally involved in his political organization, she worked in his early campaigns when the only organization he had was his congregation. She has watched the church change and grow, and she feels it is going in the direction that Adam wished it would. Since his death, Miss Jones has been helping to compile memorabilia for an Adam Clayton Powell Room at Abyssinian.

Holman McDonald

Holman McDonald is one of the leading citizens of Bimini. He began in construction and stonemasonry, and now he operates a small grocery business. Mr. McDonald is very concerned with education—his wife is assistant principal of the school and he is on the school board— with the independence of the Bahamas, and with the general betterment of life on Bimini. He and Adam Powell frequently discussed these things.

Adam Clayton Powell, III (Skipper Powell)

Skipper Powell is the son of Adam Powell and Hazel Scott. A graduate of Massachusetts Institute of Technology, he has made his own way in electronics, and in radio and television, and though he has not carried on family traditions either in the church or in politics, he has carried on the famous family name. His son is Adam Clayton Powell, IV.

Emmanuel Rolle

One of the more prosperous Bimini residents, Emmanuel Rolle owns a deep-sea fishing boat, which he charters by the day to tourists, and also owns a grocery store. He and Adam shared many good times fishing.

Pearl Swangson

As secretary–hairdresser–Girl Friday to Hazel Scott, Pearl Swangson knew Adam Powell very well. She traveled to Europe with the family and lived with them while they were in the United States. Even after Adam and Hazel Scott were divorced, Adam remained in close contact, and Pearl Swangson saw him several times during his last two years. Many say that of all the women in his life Adam loved Hazel Scott most. Pearl Swangson, perhaps more than anyone else, had the opportunity to see them together.

Lewis Upshur

Lewis Upshur was with Adam Powell from the beginning of Adam's career in public life. When he and Lillian Upshur were married in 1947, he had already known Adam for fifteen years. After that, the Upshurs together worked for him. In 1932 Lewis Upshur heard Adam preach and vowed he was going to follow him everywhere; now that Adam is gone, Lewis Upshur, more than most others, keeps his memory alive.

Lillian Upshur

Lillian Upshur's family were members of Abyssinian, but she did not know Adam Powell well until, fresh out of college, he began to take an active role in Abyssinian Baptist Church. From that time she watched him grow as a man, and she helped him grow as a politician. She was his secretary first and then an important organizer of nearly all his successful political campaigns. After Adam Powell died, Lillian Upshur was one of the people who carried his ashes to Bimini.

Appendix B

The legislative record of Representative Adam Clayton Powell, Chairman, Committee on Education and Labor, United States House of Representatives

Public
Law   *Title*

          87th Congress   [1961-1963]

87-22   Amending vocational education laws to include and help practical nurse training programs.

87-30   Increasing the coverage of minimum wage legislation to include retail clerks; also increasing the minimum wage to $1.25.

87-87   Increased benefits for longshoremen and harbor workers.

87-137   Provides for one additional Assistant Secretary of Labor.

87-262   Establishes a teaching hospital for Howard University, transfers Freedmen's Hospital to Howard University.

87-274   The Juvenile Delinquency and Youth Offenses Control Act.

87-276   Providing for the training of teachers of the deaf and handicapped children.

87-294   Education of the blind.

87-300   Study of health and safety conditions in metal mines.

87-344   Extension of the laws providing funds for school construction and maintenance in federally impacted areas.

87-399   Amending the Federal Employee's Compensation Act.

87-400   Amending the National Defense Education Act regarding student loans.

87-415   The Manpower Development and Training Act, to make more jobs available.

87-420   Amending the Welfare and Pension Plans Disclosure Act.

87-581   The Work Hours Act of 1962, establishing standards for pay and work of laborers and mechanics.

87-715   Educational and training films for the deaf.

87-729   Amending the Manpower Development and Training Act regarding railroad unemployment insurance.

87-823   Liberalizing formula under National School Lunch Act.

88-38   Equal pay for equal work.

88-204   Higher Education Academic Facilities Act.

88-210   Improving the quality of vocational education, providing for its expansion and strengthening.

88-214   Amending the Manpower and Development Training Act.

88-269   Increasing Federal assistance for public libraries.

88-321   President's Committee on Employment of the Physically Handicapped.

88-349   Amending the prevailing wage section of the Davis-Bacon Act.

88-368   Amending the Juvenile Delinquency and Youth Offenses Control Act of 1961 by extending it for two more years.

88-444   National Commission on Technology, Automation, and Economic Progress.

88-452   The War on Poverty.

88-508   Amending the Federal Employees Compensation Act.

88-579   National Council on the Arts.

88-582   Registration of contractors of migrant workers.

88-665   Amending and extending the National Defense Education Act of 1958.

89th Congress   [1965-1967]

89-10   Improving elementary and secondary educational opportunities.

89-15   Amending the Manpower Development and Training Act of 1962.

89-36   National Technical Institute for the Deaf.

89-69   Amending the Juvenile Delinquency and Youth Offenses Control Act of 1961.

89-73   The Older Americans Act of 1965.

89-77   Amending Public Law 815, providing for school construction in Puerto Rico, Wake Island, Guam and the Virgin Islands.

89-125   Amending the National Arts and Cultural Development Act of 1964.

89-178   Providing for analysis of manpower shortage in correctional rehabilitation.

89-133   Providing for assistance in construction and operation of public elementary and secondary schools in areas affected by major disaster.

89-209   National Foundation on the Arts and the Humanities.

89-216   Bonding Provisions of Labor-Management Reporting and Disclosure Act of 1959.

89-239   Strengthening the educational resources of our colleges and univerities; and to financially assist such students.

89-253   Expanding the War on Poverty.

89-258   Expansion of loan service of educational media for the deaf.

89-286   Labor standards for persons employed by Federal contractors.

89-287   Financial assistance for students attending trade, technical, business, and other vocational schools, after secondary education.

89-333   Amending the Vocational Rehabilitation Act.

89-376   Coal mine safety.

89-448   Federal Employees Compensation Act Amendments of 1966.

89-511   Extend and amend Library Services and Construction Act.

89-577   Metallic and nonmetallic mine safety.

89-598   International Education Act of 1966.

89-601   Fair Labor Standards Act Amendments of 1966.

89-694   Model secondary school for the deaf.

89-750   Elementary and secondary education amendments of 1966.

89-752   Higher Education Act of 1966.

89-792   Manpower Development and Training Act Amendments of 1966.

89-794   Economic Opportunity Act Amendments of 1966.

Index

172]

About the Author

James Haskins is the author of a number of adult and young adult books, including *A Piece of the Power: Four Black Mayors; Diary of a Harlem Schoolteacher; Profiles in Black Power;* and *The Psychology of Black Language* (with Hugh F. Butts, M.D.). He is a professor in the experimental college at Staten Island Community College and a member of the faculty of the graduate school of education at Manhattanville College. He lives in New York City.